The Easy Harvest
Sauce & Puree Cookbook

Marjorie Blanchard

Garden Way Publishing ✾ Pownal, Vermont 05261

Illustrations by Carol MacDonald
Chapter opening photos by Ray Cicero

Library of Congress Cataloging in Publication Data

Blanchard, Marjorie P.
  The easy harvest sauce and puree cookbook.

  Reprint. Originally published: Sauce it. Charlotte, Vt. : Garden Way
Publishing, c1979.
  Includes Index
  1. Sauces. 2. Cookery (Fruit) 3. Cookery (Vegetables) I. Title.
TX819.A1B55 1980   641.8'14   82-934
ISBN 0-88266-272-4   AACR2

Contents

Introduction

A fine sauce will make even an elephant palatable." This was spoken in jest perhaps, but the author of this little maxim (de la Reyniere) was a Frenchman, and it is to the French that we owe our present repertoire of classic sauces, and their uses.

Actually, what is a sauce? It is any soft or liquid dressing that accompanies food — anything that adds zest, flavor, or piquancy. A sauce should enhance the flavor of a dish. It may be an essential part of that dish or only an accompaniment, but it should at the same time be worth eating by itself. A sauce is not a blanket intended to cover or smother.

Sauces have come a long way since the days of the Romans when they had absolutely no relation to the foods they accompanied and the flavors were so strong that they turned birds into fish and meats into birds. This may have been all to the good in some cases, although there are not many palates today that would have relished "garum," one of the earliest and best known of sauces. It was an extract of juices from fish of the mackerel family with additives of honey, vinegar, fish livers, and anchovy puree — a bit strong for our tastes but it probably covered a multitude of sins.

The Middle Ages also brought strong sauces, very heavy on the salt and pepper and spices and generally too sweet. For instance, a sauce for roast beef was made of apples, raisins, pepper, nutmeg, ginger, sugar, and port wine. Of course, we don't know what their roast beef was like but that sauce certainly would have overpowered ours.

As early as the 14th century, there were professional saucemakers in Paris, but it was the arrival of Catherine de Medici with her Italian chefs that earned French cuisine its first stars. This was the middle of the 16th century and the saucepot boiled and bubbled from then on. Unfortunately, its contents did not apparently reach much beyond the continent's borders because some 250 years later someone made the remark that "while England has many religions, it still has only one sauce."

In America, we relied on English cookbooks in our colonial era. Most of our sauces were just the liquids formed during the cooking process, as in stews. They were not thickened but served with dry toasted bread. The best kitchens, however, did use egg yolks, butter, and cream — probably far more than we do today — and there is a mention of onion sauce in the first cookbook ever printed in this country. (Amelia Simmons, 1796.)

In 1837 Miss Leslie's book, *Directions for Cookery*, had a whole chapter on sauces and how to keep them. From there on we find a lot of attention being paid to sauces and a ruinous overemphasis on the recipe known then as White Sauce. Think of all the meals that ended up being white all over! Thankfully, since then we have found that sauces can be made of many different things — and can be used over, in, or about foods.

In this book we have tried to gather together all of the possible sauces made from fruits and vegetables — excluding those things that do not lend themselves logically to being sauce material. Beets, for instance. Or green peppers. We hope to help you extend the uses of your garden and orchard produce, as well as stimulate your kitchen creativity. Sauces are easy to make and to store, canned or frozen or dried. They can be the basis of a good dish or the final touch that makes a dish outstanding. We all think of tomatoes and apples when we think sauce, but did you ever try rhubarb sauce on pork, cucumber sauce on fish, or zucchini sauce on chicken? The alliums — onions, garlic, shallots and leeks — make delicious sauces that can be turned into soups, and the herb garden will yield innumerable ideas for butter sauces that can be frozen for future use. The berry patch, the grape vine, and even your nut trees will produce sauces to use that surplus with which we all have to cope in a good growing year.

To be a true sauce, the fruit or vegetable must be pureed and flavored so that it will stand on its own, if necessary. By doing this bit of preparation, you can use the sauce as a base for many recipes such as cakes, puddings, soufflés, custards, and soups. Sauces are one more way of getting the most out of your planting and the answer to using up that last bit of broccoli, pumpkin, or squash that won't quite fit into the freezer container. What's more, they add one more dimension to your cooking repertoire and meal planning — and who doesn't need that?

Lately, in the ever-changing world of cookery, pureed fruits and vegetables have been put to a new use. They are being used as thickeners. Instead of using flour and butter to make a smooth, finished sauce, we can hold the sauce together and thicken it with its own ingredients. This is generally the technique used with gravies which are usually associated with meats and poultry. In this case, we can take a bit of creative license and thicken the vegetables surrounding the meat, fish or poultry just by pureeing them and possibly reducing the mixture.

We have given the weight or measure of each fruit and vegetable and their equivalent measures after being pureed. This is approximate, as vegetables and fruits differ in their moisture content, degree of ripeness, etc. You may find your own measurements to be slightly more or less.

Equipment
and Methods

At the risk of sounding like Pollyanna in the kitchen, I must point out how blessed today's housewife is, thanks to modern technology. Undoubtedly it is the result of constant female nagging since the days of the caveman, but we have come a long way in kitchen equipment, all designed to ease the cook's burdens since the mortar and pestle.

There are certain pieces of equipment that should be part of every serious cook's kitchen — tools that will make preparation of sauces and dressings not only easier but more professional, and the end results will be more pleasing to the palate as well as to the eye.

Old-fashioned *wooden spoons* are still important for stirring delicate sauces and it is a good idea to have an assortment. *Whisks* are also handy in various sizes and shapes, and even the rank beginner will have trouble getting lumps in a sauce or gravy that is stirred with a whisk. Incidentally, a kitchen is like any studio. It is more workmanlike and attractive if its tools are in plain view. Today the sizes and shapes of spoons, spatulas, and beaters have an esthetic beauty that adds to the overall decor of a room. Invest in one or two attractive containers for those things you use all the time and keep them on the counter within easy reach.

A lot of tools can hang on hooks or pegboard and these include *strainers*. Strainers come in a wide variety of sizes and shapes, and I shall discuss a few of the ones important to saucemaking. The words *strainer* and *sieve* are used interchangeably, but just for the record this is the difference between the two: a strainer separates liquids from solids; a sieve refines the texture of the strained material. You can ask for either one, and in today's well-stocked kitchen departments you will be faced with a bewildering display of both. Treat yourself to three sizes. As for the type, that is entirely up to your sense of economy. The tinned steel sieves are sturdier than the aluminum mesh but they rust eventually. It really is a toss-up between the two. A different breed altogether is the glamorous stainless steel sieve with steel rim and handle. These are handsome to look at and immensely professional although they have a shallower cup.

There are also sieves with nylon mesh that are used for delicate sauces such as wine sauce to avoid the risk of discoloration. You have probably seen the conical sieves called *chinois* or *rotary ricers*. These are made of both stainless and tinned steel. They are not very expensive, and my choice would be the one with the stand and wooden pestle — although it does present a bit of a storage problem. However, it is a handsome addition to any kitchen.

All of these sieves require a certain amount of hard labor, just plain pressing and pushing. They are good for small amounts of food but possibly produce more juice than actual puree. They are essential for straining food that has been pureed in a blender or food processor with the seeds.

Pressing brings up two more tools that are indispensable. One is the *garlic press* which is a very handy way of extruding pureed garlic into a dish. Just be sure you buy one that has large enough holes for unpeeled garlic cloves because that in itself is a timesaver. The other press is the old-fashioned *potato ricer*, and in case you haven't seen one lately, even this basic machine has been updated. I have a gleaming Italian stainless steel ricer that comes with two screens, so I can do either vegetables or berries just by changing the hole size. There is also on the market a bright plastic ricer that is a little less expensive and not quite as sturdy but does a perfectly adequate job. Either one is ideal for a small amount of puree.

The *food mill* is really a hand-operated mechanized sieve. It separates pulp, skin and seeds, letting the pulp go through the holes. The degree of refinement is decided by the size screen you use, and most come with at least three screens. Instead of pushing, you simply turn a handle. In spite of the new electric machines, the food mill still has a place in the kitchen and performs functions that the blender or food processor cannot. For instance, I could not make small amounts of applesauce without my food mill, because I cook the apples whole to preserve all of their flavor and nutriments and the food mill is the obvious way to process them into sauce. Again, this handles small amounts very well and gives you pulp, not juice.

There is a larger hand-operated machine that works on this same principle. It is known as an *Italian tomato machine*. It also has strainers with various sized holes (three) but will take much larger amounts of fruits and vegetables and is very handy to have when the tomato season is in full swing — and on to apples and pumpkins. If you grow these vegetables in quantity, perhaps this large machine is for you. The Squeezo Strainer version must be clamped onto a table

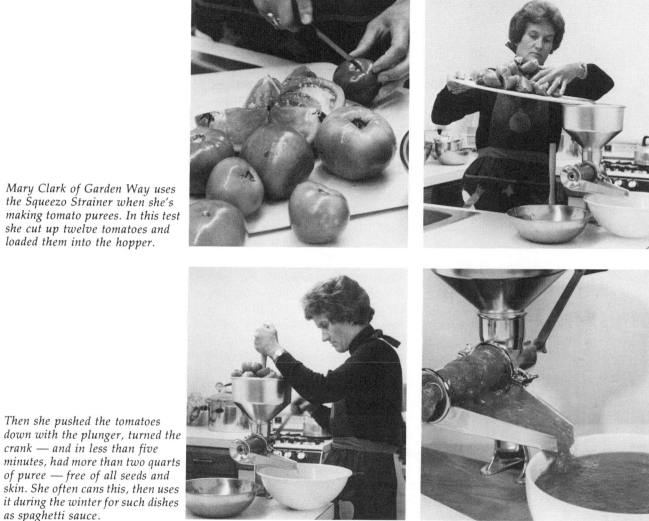

Mary Clark of Garden Way uses the Squeezo Strainer when she's making tomato purees. In this test she cut up twelve tomatoes and loaded them into the hopper.

Then she pushed the tomatoes down with the plunger, turned the crank — and in less than five minutes, had more than two quarts of puree — free of all seeds and skin. She often cans this, then uses it during the winter for such dishes as spaghetti sauce.

or counter top. There is also a tomato-red polypropylene model on the market that sticks to the counter with suction cups and comes with a square dish to catch the puree as it slides out. Either of these is essential for quantity production. The one important thing to remember about using any of these sieves or food mills is that, except for tomatoes, the vegetables and fruits should be cut up and softened by cooking for easiest processing. It's only necessary to cut up tomatoes.

Now we come to the *electrified food mills* — the first one being the *blender* which has been around for quite a while. Here again is a machine that does things the others cannot do. In some instances it will produce a finer and smoother puree than the food processor, and it can't be beaten for whipping up frothy drinks. The major problem with the blender is that it is necessary to stop and start frequently to push food down into the blades. And it does not work satisfactorily without some liquid in the mixture. However, it deserves a place in the kitchen, not high on a pantry shelf.

The *food processor* does not do everything — what does? It will not whip cream or egg whites or make decent mashed potatoes. In spite of the ads, it will not automatically turn you into a French chef, but it will cut and chop and grate with incredible speed and save important hours when you are canning and preserving. This amazing machine will inspire you to try dishes that you have not attempted before, which in turn will make your meals more exciting — and as we turn the corner in our general economy from easy affluence to careful frugality and a need to economize energy as well as cash, the electric food processor could be a worthwhile investment.

Another department of the kitchen should be mentioned — *pots and pans*. Aluminum has fallen from grace with many cooks because it imparts a poor color and flavor to acid foods, and egg- and wine-based sauces. The material taking the place of aluminum is stainless steel which usually comes with an aluminum piece in the bottom or an aluminum-clad outside to intensify and even out the heat conduction. These pots, especially in the larger stockpot sizes, are expensive, but they are virtually a lifetime investment and to the serious cook certainly worth the money. There is also a line of black, satin-finish treated aluminum that is impervious to any chemical reaction — again, expensive. But as James Beard invariably says to the ladies, "You all think nothing of buying a new set of golf clubs, but you cook every day with the same old pans you got when you were married!"

Incidentally, the deeper the pot the less mess you will have on your stove when cooking tomatoes or applesauce, as they have a tendency to bubble over and spatter everything within range.

The final suggestion for equipment is a *scale*. I have found that the easiest and least confusing way of handling produce is simply to weigh it. Weight is the lowest common denominator and the most easily understood by everyone. The old-fashioned pecks and bushels do not hold up anymore. So get yourself a kitchen scale. You will have to have one anyhow when we change to the metric system because things like sugar and flour will be given in weight, not cups. Scales are not expensive and you will get into the habit of weighing everything that comes into the kitchen, including the cat.

Seasonings

"The harmony which strikes the eye in a picture should in a sauce cause in the palate as agreeable a sensation.".

This interesting thought comes from an introduction to a cookbook written some 200 years ago by a Jesuit priest, who was as much interested in the chemistry of food as in the eating of it. He cautions us that the two are irrevocably tied together — and seasonings are the secret of success in the art of cooking.

When ripe tomatoes are put through a food mill they come out as a tomato puree — rich with the taste of tomato but not particularly distinguished in flavor. But add a bit of oregano, some salt and pepper, a crush of garlic, a spoonful of olive oil — then taste and see what you have. This is at least a basic tomato sauce. Go further and stir in wine, basil, sautéed celery, onion, and carrot. Cook this mixture until it is soft. Strain it and you will have an excellent sauce for chicken or veal.

Make a puree of apples. Stir in a little butter, salt, and lemon juice. Taste.

Good but bland. Add a splash of vanilla, some cinnamon, and nutmeg. Better. Pour in some brandy and sprinkle with grated orange rind. Heat until well blended and slightly thickened. Serve with roast pork or as a tart filling in a walnut crust. With judicious seasoning, you have just created a lovely dish.

Seasonings are added to foods to heighten, blend, and give depth and character to what otherwise would be a somewhat pallid, flavorless mixture. The only way we can properly handle seasonings is to taste. And the only way to taste is with an open mind, as well as a clear palate. (Don't taste if you have a cold.) Actually it is not your taste buds that are doing the work; it is your sense of smell. The taste buds in our mouths record four sensations — sweet, salt, sour and bitter. They also record texture. It is the odors of foods that create the appetite for them. Think of coffee, bacon, warm bread, applesauce simmering with cinnamon and nutmeg. The smells make you hungry, and you just hope the flavors measure up.

If you missed chemistry in school, don't be worried. In cooking you can work with a kind of chemistry that is much more fun than just lighting matches over test tubes. Putting together harmonizing flavors in food is a chemistry that takes constant experimentation but is totally rewarding, because it is very personal. You can put in what you like and take out what you don't like. It is all a matter of taste — your own.

Before you use an herb that is called for in a recipe, taste it. If it is a strong herb such as rosemary, use a very small amount. (In Italy, rosemary branches are used to brush oil over a leg of lamb as it cooks). Parsley can be used liberally, as it has a definite but not overpowering flavor. Each allium has a personality all its own, and if you nibble on raw chives, leeks, or shallots you will see why they are used differently with various foods. Also, there is a great difference between fresh and dried herbs. The general rule of thumb is three times the amount of fresh as dried in a recipe. When an herb is dried, it increases in intensity.

Just one word of caution in using seasonings — don't overdo a good thing. I remember many years ago having dinner with a young man who was new to cooking but determined to give it his all. In this case his all was curry powder and everything we ate was liberally doused with curry including the peas. He even put the bottle of curry powder on the table. This produces what I call food fatigue and too much of anything may turn you off that particular seasoning forever.

When using both herbs and spices, the process of bruising the seasoning is essential to bring out the full volatile oils. With herbs, this is a case of pounding in a mortar or chopping fine. If the herbs are dried, rub them between your fingers. With spices, grind the whole spice just before you use it. We have found that little boxes of spices sitting on the shelf year in and year out lose most of their pungency and are dry as dust after a time. Most spices — allspice, cloves, cinnamon, nutmeg, cardamom, cumin — can be purchased whole. There is now on the market a very neat little hand-operated spice grinder that makes quick work of grinding just the amount of spice you need for a recipe. There is nothing more fragrant than fresh-ground spices. They perfume the whole kitchen. Incidentally, in colonial times, whole cloves were frequently burned to remove odors in the room.

Make your own seasoning combinations — seasoned salt, for instance, or curry powder, or Chinese five spices. They will be fresher and less expensive than anything you can buy. Keep them in tightly stoppered glass bottles in a cool cupboard. You can dry your herbs in a dehydrator and package them in small jars or cloth bags. You can even make your own tea bags using home-grown herbs.

When working with seasonings, remember that subtlety is the secret. You are trying to blend and meld and point up the true flavors of a dish. When using fresh garden produce, it is especially important to keep the flavor of the fruit or vegetable dominant. We have come a long way from the days when seasonings

were used to cover up unsavory foods. Above all, don't be afraid to experiment. When you make a large batch of tomato or applesauce, put small amounts into separate bowls and season each one differently. Call in volunteers for tasting and take a vote. Then go on to season the larger amount that will be preserved for future use. Your kitchen will be more fascinating than any chemistry lab and just as productive — and your own sense of taste will be heightened and refined.

CHINESE FIVE SPICES

Equal parts:

Cinnamon, clove, fennel, anise, black pepper

Grind together and store in airtight jar. Use as poultry seasoning, in soups, stews, casseroles.

HERB MIX

6 tablespoons dried parsley
1 tablespoon dried thyme
2 bay leaves, crushed
½ tablespoon dried marjoram
1 tablespoon dried basil
½ teaspoon pepper

Mix all together and store in airtight container or put in small cloth bags, 1 tablespoon in each.

CURRY POWDER

3 ounces whole coriander
3 ounces ground turmeric
1 ounce each whole peppercorns, mustard seed, ginger
½ ounce each whole allspice and cardamom
¼ ounce whole cumin

Weigh spices and grind. Mix together, blending thoroughly.

Preserving Purees

What's your favorite method of preserving foods? Canning? Freezing? Drying? Any of these methods (with some limitations) can be used for saving purees for later use.

Canning

Fruit purees can be canned using the boiling water bath method. They should be processed for an average of fifteen minutes in the boiling water. Leave a quarter inch of head space in the jar.

Corn syrup or honey may be substituted for sugar in fruit purees. Up to one-third of the sugar may be replaced with corn syrup. Up to half the sugar may be replaced with honey. However, remember that honey has a definite flavor all its own, and your strawberries may come through tasting of wild thyme or clover.

Except for tomatoes, we do not advise canning any *vegetable* purees. Not

enough definitive research has been done in this field, so we're being very careful. The problem is that because of the greater density involved in a puree as compared to whole vegetables, there is no guarantee that the puree will can perfectly.

Freezing

As a substitute for canning vegetable purees, we can freeze them. This is easier and certainly safer and also keeps the natural color of the food better than any other method of preservation. Points to remember when freezing:

- Start with a high quality product.
- Prepare under sanitary conditions.
- Use proper packaging — containers that are moisture-proof and capable of being tightly closed.
- Store like foods together.
- Turnover is the key to economy in frozen food so keep replacing the foods as you use them, moving containers from back to front in the freezer.
- Keep a record of frozen foods with dates.
- Freeze as quickly as possible after processing.
- Check your freezer to make sure the temperature maintains zero degrees or lower.

Plastic freezer boxes, freezer jars with wide mouths, flexible bags, and plastic wrap can be used when freezing purees. If you do a lot of freezing, it is easier to purchase these in large quantities. Buy a roll of plastic wrap at a restaurant supply house. You may wish to invest in a gadget that seals plastic bags and also a vacuum freezer pump that removes air from the package.

To freeze vegetable purees: after preparing puree, cool it as quickly as possible by immersing container of puree in ice water. Pack into freezer container leaving a half-inch head space. Seal, label, and date. Purees can be kept for one year without loss of flavor.

To freeze fruit purees: follow directions for vegetable purees above. The addition of lemon juice or ascorbic acid while preparing purees is only to retain the true color. The amount of sweetening can be added according to taste.

Drying

When fruit or vegetable purees are dehydrated, they are appropriately called leathers, because the result is a sheet of a leathery substance that can be stored in rolls or strips, or can be put into a blender and powdered, then stored.

TOMATO LEATHER: Spread puree a quarter-inch deep on plastic wrap over tray in dehydrator. Dry 6-8 hours. Dry until brittle if you wish to make a powder. Use powder for soups, juices or sauce flavoring. You can add herbs and spices to the puree before drying.

FRUIT LEATHERS: Use single fruits or combinations of two or more. These fruit leathers can be eaten as candy, or blended into powder and used to flavor ice cream, puddings, yogurt, dessert toppings or tarts.

To store leathers:

For short-term storage, leathers can be rolled up on plastic wrap.

For long-term storage (one to two years) they should be stored flat between sheets of brown paper. Or you can cut them into short lengths and store in tightly closed glass jars.

Just make sure they are in a dry, dark, and cool place. This also applies to the powdered leathers. Small amber or green glass jars with airtight stoppers are ideal for these powders. Keep the jars in a cupboard.

Dehydrating food is fun and well worth experimenting with. If you have the equipment, by all means try it.

Traditional Sauces

BÉARNAISE SAUCE

½ cup dry white wine
2 tablespoons tarragon vinegar
1 tablespoon minced shallots
2 sprigs chopped tarragon
1 sprig chopped parsley
3 egg yolks
1 tablespoon lemon juice
½ cup butter
1 tablespoon chopped chives
½ teaspoon salt

Combine in heavy saucepan the wine, vinegar, shallots, tarragon, and parsley. Bring to a boil and boil rapidly until liquid is reduced to half. Set aside.

In small saucepan put yolks and lemon juice. Stir over lowest heat adding butter bit by bit until mixture is thick and smooth. Stir in reduced liquid and chives. Season to taste.

Serve over beef.

Variation:

CHORON SAUCE: Add ¼ cup tomato puree and serve over meat, chicken, or fish.

BÉCHAMEL SAUCE

2 tablespoons butter
2 tablespoons flour
1 cup milk

The classic white or cream sauce has endless variations. The main point to accomplish when making this sauce is to remove any raw floury taste. This is done by cooking the roux, or butter and flour mixture, before adding the liquid.

Heat butter and flour in heavy saucepan and cook over medium high heat, stirring constantly with whisk, for 3-4 minutes. Mixture will be golden and bubbly.

Add milk all at once and cook, stirring, until mixture comes to a boil and is smooth and thick. Remove and season to taste.

Variations:

If sauce is to be used with chicken, use half chicken broth in liquid.

If sauce is to be used with fish, use half fish stock or clam broth in liquid.

NEWBURG SAUCE: To 1 cup Béchamel beat in 2 beaten yolks, 2 tablespoons sherry and 1 teaspoon dry mustard.

HORSERADISH SAUCE: To 1 cup Béchamel add 3 tablespoons prepared horseradish, 2 tablespoons heavy cream, 1 teaspoon sugar, 1 teaspoon mustard, and 1 teaspoon vinegar.

EGG SAUCE (for salmon): To 1 cup Béchamel add 2 chopped hardcooked eggs, 1 tablespoon capers, 1 tablespoon chopped dill.

MORNAY SAUCE: To 1 cup Béchamel add 1 egg yolk and 4 tablespoons grated cheese.

SAUCE SUPREME: Replace ¼ cup milk with white wine and add 1 teaspoon brandy. Use over poached chicken breasts.

SAUCE AURORE: To 1 cup Béchamel, add ½ cup tomato puree and 1 tablespoon butter. Serve over fish.

BLENDER MAYONNAISE

1 whole egg
1 teaspoon dry mustard
1 teaspoon salt
1½ cups salad oil
2 tablespoons lemon juice

Put in container of blender or food processor the egg, mustard, salt, and ¼ cup oil. Turn motor on and off to mix. Turn motor on and add slowly ½ cup oil, dripping in a steady stream until mixture starts to thicken. Add lemon juice and blend thoroughly. Add remaining oil slowly and blend until thick. Taste for seasoning. If mixture curdles or refuses to thicken, pour from container to bowl. Thoroughly wash and dry container. Put 1 yolk into container and blend, slowly adding curdled mixture. It should come together.

BLENDER MUSHROOM SAUCE

¼ pound mushrooms
½ cup sour cream
½ cup beef bouillon
2 tablespoons butter
2 tablespoons flour
Salt and pepper to taste

Place all ingredients in container of blender or food processor. Process briefly.
Turn out into heavy saucepan and cook over medium heat, stirring, until thickened. Serve over meat loaf, broiled chicken, or cheese soufflé.

CUSTARD SAUCE

3 egg yolks
1 cup milk
½ cup sugar
1 teaspoon vanilla

Combine yolks, milk, and sugar in heavy saucepan. Cook over medium heat, stirring constantly, until thick and smooth. Sauce should coat back of spoon. Cool. Add vanilla. Serve over fresh or poached fruit.

FOAMY CREAM SAUCE

1 cup confectioners' sugar
1 egg yolk
1 teaspoon vanilla
1 egg white
Pinch of salt
1 cup heavy cream, whipped

Beat together the sugar, yolk, and vanilla. Beat egg white with a pinch of salt until stiff. Fold into yolk mixture. Fold in whipped cream. Serve with hot puddings or soufflés.

GRAND MARNIER SAUCE

6 egg yolks
¼ cup sugar
⅓ cup Grand Marnier or any orange liqueur
1 cup heavy cream, whipped

Beat yolks and sugar in top of double boiler until creamy. Place over hot water and beat until mixture forms a ribbon when dropped from a spoon. Remove from heat and beat until cool. Beat in liqueur gradually. Fold in whipped cream. Chill. Serve over fruit, puddings, or soufflés.

GREEN GODDESS SAUCE

1 cup mayonnaise
½ cup sour cream
1 garlic clove, minced
2 anchovy fillets, minced
¼ cup chopped chives
¼ cup minced parsley
4-5 watercress or spinach leaves, minced
2 teaspoons lemon juice
1 tablespoon herb vinegar
Salt and pepper to taste

This famous sauce comes from the Palace Court in San Francisco where it is served over crab salad. It is good on any kind of seafood or a plain green salad.

Combine all ingredients. (This can be done in a blender or food processor in which case ingredients don't have to be chopped first.)

HOLLANDAISE SAUCE

3 egg yolks
1-2 tablespoons lemon juice
    (to taste)
½ teaspoon salt
Freshly ground pepper to taste
½ cup butter cut into
    tablespoons

Put yolks and seasonings into small, heavy saucepan. Place on lowest heat. Add butter, a piece at a time, stirring constantly with a wooden spoon. When sauce is thick and smooth, turn off heat and leave in pan. If sauce has separated, rapidly stir in 1 ice cube until sauce comes together again. Serve over any hot vegetable or fish.

Variations:

MALTAISE: Substitute orange juice for lemon and add 1 teaspoon grated orange rind. Use on asparagus.
MOUSSELINE: Just before serving fold in ¼ cup whipped cream.

HONEY YOGURT SAUCE

1 cup honey yogurt
¼ cup mayonnaise
2 tablespoons herb vinegar
2 tablespoons mustard
½ teaspoon salt
1 tablespoon minced chives

Mix all ingredients together, blending well. Serve on coleslaw, potato or cooked vegetable salad.

REMOULADE SAUCE

1 cup mayonnaise
1 tablespoon drained, finely
    chopped pickle
1 tablespoon drained capers
1 teaspoon Dijon mustard
1 teaspoon minced parsley
1 teaspoon chopped chervil
½ teaspoon anchovy paste
    (optional)

Combine all ingredients. Use on shellfish or julienned celery root or turnips.

TARTAR SAUCE

1 cup mayonnaise
1 teaspoon Dijon mustard
2 teaspoons minced shallots or green onions
2 teaspoons chopped sweet pickle
1 tablespoon drained capers, chopped
2 teaspoons chopped parsley
1 chopped hardcooked egg
2 drops Tabasco sauce

Combine all ingredients. Use on fried fish or seafood.

VINAIGRETTE SAUCE

1 teaspoon salt
1 teaspoon pepper
1 teaspoon dry mustard
¼ cup herb vinegar (garlic or tarragon)
¾ cup oil

This is the classic sauce for a green salad. It can be varied by the addition of Worcestershire, chili sauce, cheese, herbs, onions, anchovies, or many other flavorings — all to your own taste. Experiment.

Put seasonings and vinegar in small bowl. Beat with fork until dissolved. Beat in oil until dressing is smooth. You may substitute lemon juice for part or all of the vinegar.

Vegetables

Asparagus

Three cups cut in ½-inch lengths equal 1 cup puree.

METHOD: Break off and discard tough bottom part of stems and cut stalks into 1-inch lengths. Cook in boiling salted water for 3-4 minutes. Drain and put through food mill or puree in blender or food processor. Asparagus puree can be frozen.

There are those who think it a sacrilege to eat asparagus any other way but in stalk form, napped with Hollandaise or a lemon-butter sauce. However, if you have a surplus of asparagus, it is nice to view it in some other fashion after it appears night after night during the height of the season. Asparagus puree makes lovely soup with a chicken stock base and the addition of potato, curry powder, and shrimp. Mixed with cream cheese, it is a flavorful stuffing for mushrooms or strudel dough. The sauce can be added to Hollandaise to serve with hot salmon or to mayonnaise to mask a cold salmon. We like asparagus as a bed for baked oysters, and our asparagus crepes can be frozen for future use.

Spread asparagus puree over the bottom of a pie shell and fill it with an onion-cheese-custard mixture — or incorporate it into a ham mousse. The mixture I use for the former is a quarter cup of sautéed onions, a half cup of grated cheese, three eggs beaten with two cups of milk, seasoned with salt, pepper and a half teaspoon of prepared mustard.

WHOLE WHEAT FILLED ASPARAGUS CREPES

20-24 Crepes (Serves 6-8)

½ cup asparagus puree
3 eggs
½ cup whole wheat flour
½ cup unbleached flour
1¼ cups milk
2 tablespoons melted butter
1 teaspoon salt

Filling:
4 tablespoons butter
4 tablespoons flour
1½ cups chicken bouillon
½ cup milk
Salt to taste
Freshly ground pepper
1 teaspoon prepared mustard
½ cup grated Gruyère cheese
1½ cups chopped cooked
   chicken and ham combined
½ cup grated Parmesan cheese

Combine all ingredients in container of blender or food processor and blend until smooth. Or put into large mixing bowl and whisk smooth. Prepare crepes or very thin 5½-inch pancakes.

Heat butter and stir in flour. Cook for 3 minutes. Add liquids and cook, stirring, until thick and smooth. Season with salt and pepper and mustard. Stir in Gruyère cheese and heat until cheese melts.

Combine chicken and ham with about half of sauce. Fill each crepe with 2 tablespoons mixture. Roll crepes and put one layer in buttered shallow baking dishes. Pour remaining sauce down center of rolled crepes and sprinkle with Parmesan cheese. Heat for 20-30 minutes in 325° F. oven.

BAKED OYSTERS AND ASPARAGUS

Serves 4

3 cups asparagus puree
Salt to taste
Freshly ground pepper to taste
24 oysters, shelled
1 cup cracker crumbs
½ cup melted butter
Juice of ½ lemon

Preheat oven to 425° F.

Season puree with salt and pepper. Spread over bottom of buttered shallow baking dish. Arrange drained oysters over puree. Mix together the crumbs, butter, and lemon juice. Spread over oysters. Bake for 10 minutes until hot and golden.

Green Beans

One pound equals ¾ cup puree.

METHOD: Top and tail beans and cut into half-inch lengths. Bring a large pot of salted water to a boil and put in beans. Boil, uncovered, for 4-6 minutes, until tender. (If beans are small, they will take less time.) Drain and dry. Put in blender or food processor and chop very fine. Beans will not dissolve into a puree unless you add additional liquid. They are better if they maintain some texture. The puree can be frozen.

The idea of making a puree from fresh green beans is a bit unusual, and I was very curious as to how it would come out — mainly because I remembered the green beans in baby food jars as not very appealing. It was a pleasant surprise to find that green beans fresh from the garden and pureed in my own kitchen are a vegetable of a different color — and texture. There is a small amount of crunch and a lot of bean flavor in this puree and, like some of the other green vegetables, when seasoned well with salt, pepper, onion or shallots, and ground nutmeg, it becomes a very versatile accompaniment to a meal.

This puree does well as a sauce for chicken or ham croquettes and makes an excellent stuffing for mushrooms or onions or tomatoes. It is very good cold as a kind of paté for crackers and a different filling for tacos when mixed with sesame seeds, green chiles, garlic, and Tabasco. It is nice to find a solution for the surplus of green beans that we all seem to have at one point during the growing season.

BAKED STUFFED MUSHROOMS

Serves 6

1 cup green bean puree
3 tablespoons ricotta cheese
1 garlic clove, crushed
Salt to taste
Freshly ground pepper to taste
2 tablespoons chopped parsley
24 large mushroom caps

Preheat oven to 400° F.

Mix together the bean puree, cheese, garlic, salt and pepper. Mix in parsley. Stuff mushroom caps with mixture. Set caps stuffed-side up in lightly oiled baking pan. Bake for 10 minutes or until hot. Serve as a first course or as a side dish with veal.

ZIPPY GREEN BEAN DIP

About 2 cups

2 cups green bean puree
2 tablespoons toasted sesame
   seeds
1 mild green chile pepper,
   minced
1 clove garlic, mashed
Salt to taste
Freshly ground pepper to taste

Combine all ingredients and let stand for 2 hours. Serve with corn chips.

This mixture may be blended with one 8-ounce package cream cheese and served as a spread for crackers or melba toast.

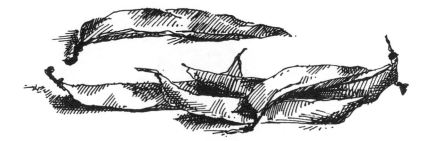

Broccoli

One pound equals 2 cups puree.

METHOD: Trim off leaves and coarsest part of stems. Cut broccoli stems into half-inch slices, leaving flowers whole. Fill a large saucepan with salted water and bring to a boil. Put broccoli into pot and boil rapidly, uncovered, for 5-10 minutes, until stems are soft. Drain in colander under cold running water. Dry. Put through food mill, or puree in blender or food processor. Can be frozen.

> Broccoli is a very rewarding vegetable because it does so many things. A plain puree seasoned with nutmeg, salt and pepper and moistened with sour cream is a good vegetable in itself, especially with turkey on Thanksgiving. Or add a little lemon juice, grated onion and chopped mild green chiles and serve with barbecued beef. And while we're on a Mexican theme, make pureed broccoli into a type of guacamole with hot chiles, Tabasco, onion, and tomatoes, and serve with corn chips.
>
> Naturally broccoli makes a handsome soufflé, especially when layered with cheese or ham or served in individual glass cups. Broccoli puree makes a nice bed for chicken breasts, and there are a variety of appropriate sauces you can use: hollandaise, béarnaise, a brown sauce, or a cheesy cream sauce. The cold ring is a new idea and can be served summer or winter, garnished with stuffed mushroom caps. Just between us, broccoli puree is a lot easier to handle than broccoli in the stalk as far as cooking and serving goes.

BROCCOLI SPOONBREAD
Serves 6-8

2 cups milk
¾ cup stoneground cornmeal
2 tablespoons butter or
    margarine
1 teaspoon salt
½ teaspoon baking powder
1 cup broccoli puree
¼ cup grated Parmesan cheese
3 eggs, separated

Preheat oven to 375° F.

Heat milk in heavy saucepan. Gradually pour in cornmeal, stirring constantly. Do not let milk boil. Cook, stirring, until thick, 7-8 minutes. Remove from heat. Stir in butter, salt, baking powder, and broccoli. Add cheese and egg yolks, mixing well. Beat egg white until stiff and fold in. Turn into well-greased 1½-quart baking dish. Bake for 40-45 minutes until firm and puffed.

COLD BROCCOLI RING
Serves 6-8

1 package plain gelatin
1 cup chicken bouillon with
    fat removed
6 hardcooked eggs, whites and
    yolks chopped separately
½ cup mayonnaise
½ cup plain yogurt or sour
    cream
1 tablespoon grated onion
1 teaspoon Worcestershire
    sauce
Dash of Tabasco
Salt to taste
Freshly ground pepper to taste
2 cups broccoli puree

Soak gelatin in ½ cup chicken bouillon. Heat remaining bouillon and dissolve gelatin until clear. Sprinkle chopped yolks in bottom of 5-cup ring mold. Pour just enough gelatin mixture over yolks to soak them. Refrigerate until firm. Mix remaining gelatin mixture with the remaining ingredients. When yolks are firm, spoon broccoli mixture into mold. Chill for several hours until firm. Turn out and serve with ham or chicken salad.

CHICKEN BREASTS OVER BROCCOLI SAUCE

Serves 4-6

3 whole chicken breasts, split,
  skinned, and boned
8 tablespoons butter
Juice of 1 lemon
1 teaspoon salt
Chicken bouillon
2 tablespoons flour
2 egg yolks
½ cup cream
3 cups broccoli puree
½ cup sour cream
½ teaspoon ground nutmeg
Salt to taste
Freshly ground pepper

Preheat oven to 425° F.

Arrange chicken breasts in one layer in buttered baking pan. Dot with 1 tablespoon butter. Sprinkle over all the lemon juice and salt. Cover tightly with aluminum foil. Bake for 12-15 minutes, until breasts are springy to the touch and white on all sides. Remove from oven and reduce heat to 325° F. Pour off and strain liquid in pan. Measure and add chicken bouillon to make 1½ cups liquid. Heat 2 tablespoons butter in saucepan and add flour. Cook stirring for 2 minutes. Add liquid (1½ cups) and cook, stirring until thickened. Beat egg yolks with cream. Remove saucepan from heat and whisk in egg mixture. Return to heat and cook, stirring until smooth and golden. Leave on simmer. Beat remaining butter and sour cream into broccoli puree. Season with nutmeg, salt and pepper. Spread puree on bottom of buttered shallow baking dish. Arrange chicken breasts over puree. Put dish in oven for 10-15 minutes to warm through. Pour sauce over all and serve.

Carrots

One pound equals 2 cups puree.

METHOD: Scrub carrots and cut into half-inch dice. Cover with salted water and bring to a boil. Cover and cook over medium heat until very tender. Drain well and puree in blender, food processor, or food mill. Scrape puree into large skillet and stir over medium heat until dry — about 2 minutes. Can be frozen.

Carrots are always with us and are a welcome sight with their vibrant color, especially in winter. They are a natural for soup just blended with chicken broth and seasonings, and sprinkled with chives. For a carrot vichysoisse, incorporate a sautéed leek and a boiled potato and serve hot or cold. Carrot soufflé or puff is light and airy. Carrot fritters are crisp and nutty, when dipped in crushed cereal flakes and sautéed. Substitute carrot for squash or pumpkin in pies and puddings. Put some pureed carrot into your next batch of doughnuts or incorporate it into waffles using buttermilk for the liquid. If you make homemade noodle dough, put some carrot puree in for a deep golden color or add it to the batter for shredded wheat muffins.

Carrot pie is the true mystery dessert. We defy anyone to guess what it is. Our carrot roulade will really help your weekly food budget. It stretches on and on.

CARROT PIE

Serves 6-8

2 cups carrot puree
3 eggs
1 cup brown sugar
¼ teaspoon salt
½ teaspoon nutmeg
¼ teaspoon ground ginger
1 teaspoon cinnamon
2 tablespoons melted butter or
    margarine
2 tablespoons light corn syrup
1 cup light cream
1 9-inch unbaked pie shell

Preheat oven to 400° F.

In large bowl beat together the carrot puree and eggs. Stir in sugar, spices, butter, corn syrup, and cream. Blend well. Pour into pie shell. Set pan on baking sheet and put on lower shelf of oven. Bake for 35-45 minutes or until firm in center. Cool to room temperature before serving.

VEAL AND CARROT ROULADE

Serves 6

½ pound ground veal
½ pound chicken, ground
    (one 1½ lb. breast)
1 egg
¼ cup bread crumbs
2 tablespoons grated onion
1 teaspoon dry mustard
Salt to taste
Freshly ground pepper
2 cups carrot puree
1 teaspoon sugar
Salt to taste
Freshly ground pepper to taste
2 tablespoons chopped parsley

Preheat oven to 350° F.

Mix together with hands the veal, chicken, egg, crumbs, onion, mustard, and salt and pepper. Mix together the carrot puree, sugar, salt, pepper, and parsley.

Spread meat mixture out on sheet of waxed paper. Cover with another sheet of waxed paper and, using rolling pin, roll out a rectangle about a half-inch thick. Remove top sheet of paper and spread meat with carrot puree. With the help of the bottom sheet of paper, roll meat up into a jelly roll and turn out onto baking sheet. Bake for 45 minutes.

To serve: slice meat and arrange slices on serving platter. Sprinkle with melted butter, lemon juice, and chopped parsley. Serve immediately or let stand and reheat before serving. Garnish with grapes.

42

Cauliflower

One medium-sized head equals 3 cups puree.

METHOD: Trim leaves and stalk off cauliflower. Separate into flowerets. Put in saucepan and fill with water halfway up side of cauliflower. Add salt. Cover and bring to a boil. Cook until very tender, 20-25 minutes. Drain and put through food mill, or puree in blender or food processor. Can be frozen.

If you are lucky enough to have cauliflower in your garden, cherish it. Many good gardeners have trouble with this vegetable and we all know that it has been a long time since we've seen any in the market at a reasonable price. Being somewhat bland in taste and appearance — actually it is one of those "either you like it or you don't" vegetables — it needs a lot of pickup and should always be served on a plate with colorful accompaniments. If you're desperate, use a lot of parsley.

Shrimp and cauliflower is an old-fashioned combination and a very agreeable one. As a soup it could be the main course of a Sunday night supper with a spinach salad and a good peppery cornbread. Apple pie for dessert?

The loaf could be part of a vegetable platter, surrounded by green beans, red beets, and orange carrots. Corned beef with pickles and mustards go well with this. All cauliflower takes is a little imagination.

CAULIFLOWER LOAF
Serves 4-6

½ cup chicken bouillon
½ cup light cream
3 eggs
1 teaspoon prepared mustard
Salt to taste
Freshly ground pepper to taste
½ cup grated Parmesan cheese
1½ cups pureed cauliflower
2 tablespoons chopped parsley
3 slices bacon, cooked and
   crumbled

Preheat oven to 375° F.

Beat together the bouillon, cream, eggs, and mustard until blended. Stir in salt, pepper, and cheese. Mix in cauliflower puree. Turn into well-buttered 1-quart deep soufflé or baking dish. Set dish in pan of hot water. Place on middle shelf of oven. Bake for 45-55 minutes until a knife inserted in edge of loaf comes out clean. Remove from oven and from pan of water. Let stand for 10 minutes. Run knife around outside edge of loaf and turn out onto serving platter. Sprinkle parsley and bacon over top.

CAULIFLOWER SOUP
Serves 4-6

¼ cup butter
2 tablespoons minced onion
¼ cup flour
3 cups chicken bouillon
2 cups whole milk
2 cups pureed cauliflower
Salt to taste
Freshly ground pepper to taste
2 tablespoons chopped toasted
   almonds
¼ cup chopped cooked shrimp

In a large saucepan heat butter. Sauté onion for 5 minutes until soft but not browned. Stir in flour and cook, stirring, for 3 minutes. Add bouillon and milk and cook, stirring, until slightly thickened. Blend in cauliflower and stir until smooth. Season with salt and pepper. Serve very hot garnished with almonds and shrimp.

Celery

One pound equals 2 cups puree.

METHOD: Cut up celery into one-inch dice, including leaves. Put in saucepan with one inch salted water in bottom. Bring to a boil, cover, and steam until tender, 20-25 minutes. Drain well. (If you use chicken broth instead of water you will add a nice flavor to the celery and have a wonderfully useful soup base.) Puree in blender or food processor. Can be frozen.

Here is another vegetable that is not found in many gardens, mainly because it is not easy to grow and takes a bit of fussing over. However, if you grow it or want to buy it in quantity when in season, puree is handy to have for that celery flavor and crunch, both of which are distinctive and unlike any other vegetable. Celery goes well with potatoes — beat it into mashed, layer it with scalloped potatoes or mix it into hash browns. A celery sauce flavored with onion and nutmeg would go nicely over a veal loaf and it makes an unusual stuffing for small fish. Cream of celery soup is a lovely way to start a meal — garnish it with chopped celery or walnuts.

Celery puree really answers the problem of wanting a bit of celery but not the whole bunch.

CELERY STUFFING FOR FISH
About 2 cups

2 tablespoons butter
1 cup pureed celery
2 tablespoons lemon juice
¼ cup minced parsley
¼ cup cream
½ cup chopped roasted
   peanuts
½ teaspoon salt
¼ teaspoon paprika

Heat butter and sauté celery for 5 minutes. Add remaining ingredients and cook over low heat for 10 minutes. Use as stuffing for small whole fish such as trout or flounder.

ROULADES OF SOLE
Serves 6

6 fillets of sole or flounder
   (approximately a
   half-pound each)
1 cup celery stuffing
Juice of 1 lemon
3 tablespoons chopped parsley
6 tablespoons butter, melted

Preheat oven to 375° F.

Butter well 12 two-inch muffin tins. Cut each fish fillet in half lengthwise. Line each muffin tin with a fillet, coiling it around to form a cup with a hole in the center. Fill the hole with celery stuffing. Place the muffin pan in a pan of hot water. Cover with waxed paper. Bake for 15-20 minutes until fish is firm and opaque. Remove from oven and let stand for 5 minutes.

With a slotted spoon remove fillets, letting them drain if necessary. Place on heated serving dish. Combine lemon juice and parsley with melted butter and pour over fish. Serve immediately.

Corn

2 cups corn kernels equals 1 cup puree.

METHOD: Cut kernels from cob and puree in blender or food processor without cooking. Can be frozen by cooking puree over medium heat for 5 minutes and adding ½ teaspoon salt to 1 cup puree.

Corn might very well be the universally most popular vegetable. There are very few people who don't like it, and even those who don't eat corn on the cob like the kernels prepared in some form or other. Puree is one more way of using corn when it is in season. With its slightly custardlike consistency, it can take the place of liquids in some recipes. Substitute corn puree for half the liquid in a cornbread or corn pudding. Add eggs and seasonings — don't forget sugar with corn — and you have a soufflé. Bind the puree with rice or breadcrumbs and use it to stuff hollowed-out tomatoes, eggplant, peppers, onions, or squashes. Bake eggs in corn with some grated cheese over the top. Make corn pancakes, crepes, or waffles, again using the puree in place of the milk. Surround a baked ham with baked apples stuffed with corn puree or make a wonderful, hearty chowder using chicken or turkey or sausages and rice. Fritters with egg yolks beaten into the puree and the whites folded in separately float from skillet to plate like feathers — and with puree in the freezer you can have them all winter long. These are just the thing for a snowy Sunday morning breakfast.

BAKED TOMATOES WITH CORN SAUCE
Serves 4

4 tablespoons vegetable oil
8 half-inch slices tomato
Salt to taste
Freshly ground pepper to taste
1 clove garlic, mashed
2 tablespoons parsley
2 eggs, separated
2 cups corn puree

Preheat oven to 375° F.

Heat oil in skillet and sauté tomato slices until just tender. They should not lose their shape. Transfer in one layer to shallow baking dish. Sprinkle with salt and pepper, garlic, and parsley. Beat yolks into corn puree. Beat whites until stiff and fold into yolk mixture. Pour over tomato slices. Bake for 25 minutes until puffy and firm. Serve immediately.

CHICKEN AND CORN CHOWDER
Serves 6-8

3 tablespoons butter or
   margarine
1 medium onion, chopped
2 medium potatoes, peeled
   and diced
6 cups chicken bouillon
Salt to taste
Freshly ground pepper to taste
2 cups corn puree
2 cups cooked diced chicken
2 cups milk or light cream
Paprika

Heat butter in heavy saucepan. Sauté onion until soft, about 5 minutes. Add potatoes and stir, coating with butter. Add bouillon, bring to a boil, and simmer covered until potatoes are tender but still firm — about 20 minutes. Season with salt and pepper. Stir in corn, chicken, and milk. Heat almost to boiling point. Serve sprinkled with paprika.

Cucumber

One pound of cucumbers equals ¾ cup puree.

METHOD: Peel, seed, and dice cucumbers. Put through food mill, or puree in blender or food processor. Drain, lightly salted, in strainer for 30 minutes. Squeeze out excess liquid. Puree can be frozen but may be watery when thawed.

Like celery, cucumbers have a distinctive flavor, subtle, but definitely in the picture. It would be best to freeze this puree as part of another dish, such as soup or with creamed chicken or chicken hash. It is also good as a filling for rolled veal scallops when mixed with ricotta cheese. Our mousse is the very breath of summer and perfect for a buffet. The dips and sauces could take a little curry powder if you are so inclined. The rolls can be made any size — even the size of bread loaves. These are fun to make and fill with egg salad, salmon, chicken, or tuna fish. Spread them with an herb butter first.

CUCUMBER SAUCE

About 2 cups

1 cup cucumber puree
½ cup sour cream
½ cup mayonnaise
Juice of ½ lemon
1 teaspoon chopped tarragon
1 teaspoon sugar
Salt to taste
Freshly ground pepper to taste

Combine all ingredients and chill well. Serve very cold over baked fish steaks or broiled chicken.

CUCUMBER ROLLS

About 2½ dozen rolls

1 package yeast
1 teaspoon sugar
¼ cup lukewarm water
½ cup cucumber puree, well
　　drained
1 cup cottage cheese (large
　　curd)
1 teaspoon salt
1 egg
6 tablespoons soft butter or
　　margarine
1 teaspoon dried dill weed *or* 1
　　tablespoon minced fresh dill
3½-4 cups unbleached flour

Add yeast and sugar to water and let stand for 5 minutes, until bubbling. In large bowl put cucumber, cottage cheese, salt, egg, and butter. Beat all together. Add dill and yeast. Stir in 3½ cups flour. Beat well. Turn out onto floured board and knead until smooth and light. Add remaining flour if needed. Dough should no longer be sticky but not as stiff as bread dough. Turn into greased bowl. Cover and let stand in warm place until doubled in bulk. Punch down and shape into rolls. Place in buttered muffin tins. Let rise again until doubled. Bake for 20-30 minutes at 350° F. until golden.

CUCUMBER MOUSSE
Serves 6

2 packages unflavored gelatin
¼ cup cold water
1 cup cucumber puree
1 tablespoon lemon juice
1 teaspoon salt
1 cup mayonnaise
Dash of Tabasco
½ cup heavy cream, whipped

In a cup soak gelatin in cold water. When gelatin is set, place cup with gelatin in a pan of simmering water and allow to melt until clear and liquid. In bowl combine cucumber puree, lemon juice, gelatin, salt, mayonnaise, and Tabasco. Fold in whipped cream. Turn into 1-quart mold or ring mold rinsed with cold water. Chill for several hours until firm. Unmold onto serving platter and garnish with greens and thin slices of cucumber.

CUCUMBER DIP
About 3 cups

2 cups cucumber puree
8 slices bacon, fried until
  crisp, and crumbled
½ cup sour cream
½ cup mayonnaise
1 teaspoon salt
2 tablespoons chopped chives
2 tablespoons chopped parsley
4 hardcooked eggs, chopped
  very fine

Mix all together and serve with crackers or melba toast.

Eggplant

One pound equals ¾ cup puree.

METHOD: Cut eggplant in half lengthwise and scoop out pulp, leaving a very thin skin. (If you do not wish to use the skin for filling, you can be more ruthless in your scooping.) Put pulp in saucepan with about a half inch of salted water in bottom. Cover and steam for 10 minutes until very soft. Drain in strainer, pressing out excess liquid, and mash with fork. To freeze, add a small amount of lemon juice.

Eggplant may be the black beauty of the garden when on the vine but it is far from handsome when cooked. However, it takes to strong seasonings and combines well with many meats and other vegetables. Season the puree with garlic, cumin or cinnamon, lemon rind, basil, parsley, or chives. Use it as stuffing for tomatoes, with some bread crumbs for body. Mix the seasoned sauce with pureed tomatoes and use over meat loaf or lamburgers or as a sauce for pasta. An eggplant soufflé is a delightful surprise for your menus, and the shrimp dish makes good use of the vegetable's Mediterranean origins.

EGGPLANT SAUCE FOR ROAST CHICKEN

About 3 cups

3 tablespoons butter
3 tablespoons flour
1 teaspoon salt
Freshly ground pepper to taste
1 teaspoon chopped chives
1 teaspoon grated lemon rind
2 cups eggplant puree
1½ cups light cream
3 tablespoons grated mild
cheddar cheese

Heat butter and add flour to pan. Cook, stirring, for 3 minutes over medium heat. Remove from heat and add salt, pepper, chives, and lemon rind. Return to heat and mix in eggplant puree. Add cream gradually, stirring until mixture is smooth and velvety. Stir in cheese. Serve hot.

EGGPLANT SOUFFLÉ

Serves 4

2 tablespoons butter
2 tablespoons minced onion
2 tablespoons flour
½ cup chicken bouillon
½ cup whole milk
3 egg yolks
2 tablespoons grated Parmesan
cheese
1 cup finely crushed cracker
crumbs (soda crackers or
saltines)
¾ cup eggplant puree
Salt to taste
Freshly ground pepper to taste
4 egg whites

Preheat oven to 350° F.

Heat butter in saucepan. Add onion and sauté for 3 minutes. Stir in flour and cook, stirring, for 3 minutes. Add bouillon and milk. Cook over medium heat until thick. Beat in egg yolks, one at a time, blending well. Stir in cheese and crumbs. Fold in eggplant. Season to taste with salt and pepper. Beat egg whites until stiff and fold in. Turn mixture into greased 1½-quart soufflé dish. Bake for 35-45 minutes until puffed and firm. Serve immediately.

GREEK EGGPLANT DISH
Serves 4

1 pound raw shrimp (2 cups cooked and shelled)
2 tablespoons vegetable oil
2 medium onions, chopped
1 clove garlic, minced
2 medium green peppers, seeded and diced
¼ cup cooked rice
½ cup tomato sauce
3 tablespoons chopped parsley
1 teaspoon basil
½ teaspoon thyme
1½ cups eggplant puree
Salt to taste
Freshly ground pepper to taste
¼ pound feta cheese

Preheat oven to 350° F.

Cook shrimp and set aside. Heat oil in large skillet and add onion, garlic, and peppers. Sauté until soft, about 10 minutes. Stir in rice, tomato sauce, herbs, seasoning, and eggplant puree. Add shrimp. (If large, cut in half.) Crumble feta cheese with fingers and stir in. Pile mixture into eggplant shells. Set shells in lightly oiled baking dish. Bake for 30 minutes.

To make eggplant shells: halve eggplant lengthwise. Scoop out flesh leaving ½-inch rim on sides. Sprinkle with lemon juice.

Garlic

One-half pound equals ½ cup puree. One-half teaspoon puree equals 1 clove.

METHOD: Blanch cloves by dropping them into boiling water for 3 minutes. Drain and skins will slip off. Put a half-pound garlic cloves in blender or food processor with 2 tablespoons oil. Puree. Can be frozen but keeps for 2-3 weeks in refrigerator.

We first planted garlic because someone told us it would keep the aphids off the roses. It does and keeps a lot of other unwelcome insects out of the garden too. It also spreads like mad and we have more than our quota of garlic every year. However, it can go into almost everything so we don't worry about its proliferation. Garlic puree is a very handy thing to have, because it means you don't have to chop a clove of garlic every time you need a bit of it. A nice trick to get just a hint of garlic in vegetables or pasta or rice is to drop a bit of puree in the cooking water. We could write a book (someone has) on the uses of garlic from soup to nuts, but we're really concentrating on sauces, so we will suggest two that can be the focal point of a whole meal. These can be strictly vegetarian meals or you can add fish. Serve a good dry white wine, bread, and fruit for dessert. It will make a different, and interesting, dinner party.

AIOLI SAUCE
About 1½ cups

1 egg
1 tablespoon vinegar
1 teaspoon salt
Freshly ground pepper to taste
1½ cups vegetable oil (or half olive oil)
3 teaspoons garlic puree

Put egg in container of blender, food processor or mixer bowl. Quickly beat in vinegar, salt and pepper. With machine running, add oil in a steady stream, very gradually incorporating oil into egg. When all of the oil has been added, beat in the garlic. You will have a thick mayonnaise sauce.

Note: This sauce and Skordalia Sauce are to be used as the focal points of simple, largely vegetable dinners. Serve platters of fresh vegetables, cooked or raw, and cooked seafood and fish such as cod, haddock, or halibut. The fish and vegetables can be dipped into the sauce. Accompany with French bread. This is only for garlic lovers.

BAGNA CAUDA
About 1 cup

½ cup butter
¼ cup vegetable oil
3 teaspoons garlic puree
1 2-ounce can flat anchovy fillets, minced
½ cup finely chopped walnuts

In a heavy saucepan over very low heat cook butter, oil, and garlic puree for 10 minutes. Do not let garlic brown. Stir in anchovy fillets and cook until they dissolve. Stir in walnuts. Place mixture over candle heater or very low flame of chafing dish stand. Surround with platters of sliced raw vegetables, including small boiled potatoes, for dipping into sauce.

PESTO SAUCE
Serves 4

1 cup basil leaves, firmly
   packed
2 teaspoons garlic puree
1 tablespoon pine nuts or
   walnuts
¼ cup Parmesan cheese
1 cup vegetable oil

Put basil, garlic, nuts, and cheese into container of blender or food processor. Start motor and gradually add oil. Blend until mixture is a smooth puree. Use as a sauce over pasta.

Note: This is very good on baked potatoes or the plain hamburger.

SKORDALIA SAUCE
About 2 cups

4 teaspoons garlic puree
2 cups potato puree
1 cup vegetable oil
Juice of 2 lemons
Salt to taste
Freshly ground pepper to taste

Beat garlic into warm potatoes. Gradually beat in oil and lemon juice, adding in small amounts and beating well between additions. Season with salt and pepper.

Lettuce

One pound equals 1½-2 cups puree depending on variety.

METHOD: Shred lettuce in narrow ribbons using food processor or chopping by hand. Drop in large pan of boiling, salted water for 2-3 minutes. Drain and dry. Does not freeze well.

No matter how carefully we plant lettuce, it seems to come in great abundance once it gets going. We can have salads three times a day and not make a dent in the crop, and in June and early July the green leafy heads are a thing of beauty in the garden. Then the heat sets in and we must eat faster and faster, more and more salads before it all bolts. This is the time when a few recipes for cooked lettuce come in handy.

In Europe it is not uncommon to be served lettuce as a hot vegetable. The trick is to serve it dry, not watery, but by shredding and blanching it first we can accomplish this. Believe it or not, a lettuce soup garnished with grated cheese and served with crusty bread and fruit makes a filling summer lunch — and there is nothing wrong with using lettuce as you would spinach or chard, as a base for gratin dishes.

The old French method of cooking new peas with shredded lettuce does credit to both vegetables.

You might also try sautéing shredded lettuce in bacon drippings with some onion and chopped green pepper, then stirring in cooked rice, tomato puree, and seasonings. Cook together until well blended. Serve with bacon or ham. Who knows, next year you may find yourself reserving a section of the garden just for "cooking" lettuces.

POACHED EGGS WITH LETTUCE AND MUSHROOMS
Serves 4

6 tablespoons butter
½ pound mushrooms,
    chopped fine
2 cups shredded lettuce
¼ cup cream
Salt to taste
Freshly ground pepper to taste
4 poached eggs
¼ cup grated Gruyère cheese

Heat butter in large skillet and add mushrooms. Stir over medium high heat for 2 minutes. Add lettuce and cook until mixture is soft. Add cream and cook until all ingredients are well blended and much of the moisture has evaporated, about 10 minutes. Season to taste and turn into shallow baking dish. Make 4 hollows in mixture and drop in the poached eggs. Sprinkle cheese over all. Brown quickly under broiler and serve immediately. Nice for brunch with grilled bananas and corn muffins.

LETTUCE SOUP
Serves 6

4 tablespoons butter
2 tablespoons chopped
    shallots
1 leek, chopped (white part
    only)
2 cups lettuce puree
6 cups chicken bouillon
½ cup rice (not minute rice)
Salt and freshly ground
    pepper to taste
1 egg yolk
½ cup cream
2 tablespoons lemon juice
Dash of Tabasco

Heat butter in saucepan and sauté shallots and leek until limp, about 5 minutes. Stir in lettuce puree and cook for 3 minutes. Add bouillon and bring to a boil. Reduce heat to medium. Cover pan and cook for 10 minutes. Add rice and cook until rice is tender. Season with salt and pepper. Remove from heat. Beat egg yolk with cream and add to soup, stirring rapidly to prevent egg from curdling. Add lemon juice and Tabasco. Return to heat and heat through. Serve with bread and cheese.

Onions

One pound equals 1 cup puree.

METHOD: Peel and slice onions. Put in large skillet or saucepan with a small amount of water and steam, covered, over low heat until very tender, about 20 minutes. Drain. Puree in blender or food processor or put through food mill. Drain. Can be frozen, and will keep in refrigerator for several days.

The idea behind making an onion puree is basically to save time, as well as onions. When you see an onion start to "go," puree it. With onion puree handy, you will save yourself the time and tears involved when you need a bit, or a lot, of onion flavoring in cooking.

You can mix up a very handy sauce by combining half onion and half tomato puree, seasoning to taste with sugar, vinegar, salt and pepper. A couple of spoonfuls of this mixture adds a lot of zip to vegetables and soups or sauces for chicken, meat loaf, or the good old hamburger. Enhanced with a lot of chopped parsley, it is very good over fish, especially cod or haddock.

Onion puree spiced with a hint of cinnamon and brown sugar is a flavorful stuffing for baked apples, to be served as an accompaniment to ham or turkey. (Pick out small apples for this.) Onion soufflé is a thing of beauty with its delicate, golden crust and an excellent foil for roast beef or steak. The famous Soubise Sauce is nothing but onion puree mixed with a basic cream sauce that is made with a stock base, instead of milk. Or you could cook rice with the puree over a very low heat until it is tender, then stir in cheese and a little cream, and serve it as a vegetable.

OEUFS A LA TRIPE
Serves 3

6 hardcooked eggs
2 cups onion puree
1 tablespoon butter or
   margarine
2 tablespoons flour
1 cup milk
1 teaspoon prepared mustard
Salt and freshly ground
   pepper to taste
¼ cup grated cheddar cheese
1 egg yolk beaten with 3
   tablespoons cream

Preheat oven to 375° F.

Slice eggs. Spread onion puree in bottom of buttered shallow baking dish. Put egg slices over onion. Heat butter in saucepan. Add flour and cook, stirring, for 3 minutes. Add milk and mustard and cook, stirring until thick and smooth. Season with salt and pepper. Stir in 2 tablespoons of the cheese and the yolk mixture. Pour sauce over eggs. Sprinkle with remaining cheese. Heat in oven for 10 minutes. Put under broiler for 2 minutes or until lightly browned.

ONION CHEESE BREAD
Serves 6-8

1 cup stoneground cornmeal
1 cup unbleached flour
2 tablespoons sugar
1 teaspoon baking powder
½ teaspoon salt
1 egg
1 cup corn puree
3 tablespoons melted
   shortening
1 cup sour cream
1 cup onion puree
½ cup grated cheddar cheese

Preheat oven to 400° F.

In a large bowl mix together the cornmeal, flour, sugar, baking powder, and salt. Beat in the egg, corn puree, and shortening. Turn into greased 9-inch square baking pan. Stir together the sour cream and onion puree. Spread over top. Sprinkle with cheese. Bake for 40 minutes until bread tests done. Serve warm.

Peas

One pound of peas equals 1 cup puree.

METHOD: Pod peas and put in a small amount of salted boiling water. Cook, covered, over high heat until very tender. Puree in blender or food processor. Can be frozen.

When the peas are ready, so must we be. It is a short time for harvesting this early summer crop, and we find ourselves podding peas on into the night so as not to waste any of this most delicious vegetable.

A friend mentioned that she thought it a sacrilege to puree peas until we pointed out some of the uses for this colorful "sauce" — and that we could consume just so many bowlsful of fresh peas in one week. When she had fresh pea soup for lunch, with bits of ham and garlic croutons, and delicate custardy pea timbales perched on fried toast rounds for supper (surrounding chicken breasts cooked with onion-tomato sauce), she agreed to the idea of making pea puree.

A week later our friend came back to us with a pea sauce for pasta, using shallots, grated Parmesan cheese and heavy cream. Superb! We countered with a sauce for cauliflower which, when surrounded by tiny buttered beets, is worth a whole roll of color film.

Pea pods were the surprise hors d'oeuvre at a summer wedding reception and caused almost as much comment as the meal that followed. The motto here must be, if you can't eat them, puree them.

PEA PODS
24 Tarts

1 tablespoon melted butter
2 tablespoons sour cream
1 teaspoon finely chopped
  mint
1 cup pea puree
Salt to taste
24 1½-inch tart shells, baked
  (see page 70)

Preheat oven to 350° F.
　Beat butter, sour cream, and mint into a puree. Add pea puree and salt to taste. Mix well. Fill pastry tube with mixture and pipe into tart shells. Or fill each shell with about 2 tablespoons of the mixture. Place on cookie sheets and heat in oven for 10 minutes. Serve immediately as hors d'oeuvres.

CAULIFLOWER WITH PEA SAUCE
Serves 4-6

1 medium head cauliflower
2-3 tablespoons cream
2 tablespoons butter
1 cup pea puree
¼ teaspoon nutmeg
1 teaspoon sugar
Salt to taste
Freshly ground pepper to taste
¼ cup fine bread crumbs
1 hardcooked egg yolk, sieved

Trim cauliflower, removing leaves and most of stem. Set on a steamer over boiling water and steam until stalk is tender when a knife point is inserted in it. This will take about 20-25 minutes. Remove to heated serving dish. In a small saucepan heat cream and butter. Stir in pea puree. Add seasonings. Heat almost to boiling. Mix crumbs and egg yolk. Pour pea sauce over whole head of cauliflower and sprinkle with crumb mixture. Serve immediately.

Potatoes

One pound equals 2 cups puree.

METHOD: Put whole potatoes into cold salted water. Cover pan and bring to a boil. Cook over medium heat until tender but not mushy. Time depends on size and age of potatoes. Do not use thin-skinned waxy potatoes for puree; they will become gluey. Drain potatoes and return to pot. Put over still warm burner and shake to dry out. When cool enough to handle, peel and put through food mill. Do not freeze or can.

As we have all found out through sad experience, mashed potatoes do not "hold" well. Therefore, taking a potato puree and making it into something else is probably a better way of using up old potatoes. If you really want to preserve it for any length of time, use the puree in bread or rolls. It does add a wonderful texture to baked goods. Potato puree can also be used in cakes, both white and chocolate. Pancakes made of seasoned puree, dredged lightly in flour or crumbs and sautéed in butter or bacon drippings are a good thought for a simple dinner. Or you might add some eggs and bake a potato ring or puff to serve with bright green peas and shiny glazed carrot sticks.

Incidentally, you should always warm milk or cream when adding to potato puree — the potato will be much fluffier. Small croquettes of puree can be dipped in egg, then in chopped almonds and deep-fried for a spectacular hors d'oeuvre. If you wish to add a golden glaze to potato toppings, paint with egg yolk as we do on our veal casserole.

POTATO PANCAKES
Serves 4

2 cups potato puree seasoned
   with salt and pepper
2 eggs, beaten
1 cup bread crumbs seasoned
   with 1 tablespoon each
   chopped parsley and chives
Shortening for frying

Divide potato into 8 portions, shaping into cakes. Dip cakes first into eggs, then into crumbs. Chill for 1 hour. Heat shortening for shallow frying in skillet. (About ⅛-inch deep.) Fry cakes on both sides until brown and crispy.

CHOCOLATE POTATO CAKE

½ cup shortening
1½ cups sugar
1 teaspoon vanilla
2 squares unsweetened
   chocolate melted over hot
   water
2 eggs
½ cup potato puree (hot)
1½ cups flour
2 teaspoons baking powder
½ teaspoon salt
1 cup buttermilk
½ cup coarsely chopped nuts

Preheat oven to 350° F.

Cream together the shortening and sugar until light. Beat in vanilla and chocolate. Beat in eggs. Blend in potato. Combine flour, baking powder and salt and add alternately with buttermilk. Stir in nuts. Turn into two 8- or 9-inch layer pans. Bake for 30 minutes until cake tests done. Cool in pans for 10 minutes before turning out onto rack.

POTATO PUFF
Serves 6

4 cups potato puree
1/4 cup butter or margarine
1/2 cup milk
2 eggs, separated
Salt and freshly ground
    pepper to taste
1/4 cup grated Parmesan cheese

Heat butter and milk until butter is melted. Beat into potato puree. Beat in egg yolks and seasoning. Beat whites until stiff and fold in. Turn mixture into buttered 1 1/2-quart baking dish. Sprinkle with cheese. Bake at 350° F. for 30-40 minutes until puffed and golden.

HEAVEN AND EARTH
Serves 6

4 tablespoons melted butter
2 cups potato puree
2 cups applesauce
2 tablespoons honey
1/2 teaspoon nutmeg
1/2 teaspoon salt

Preheat oven to 400° F.
Beat butter into warmed potato puree. Beat in remaining ingredients. You may want to add more sweetening. Turn mixture into buttered 1-quart baking dish. Bake for 30 minutes. Serve hot with roast pork, ham, or game.

ONIONS STUFFED WITH SWEET POTATOES
Serves 6

6 large yellow onions
1 cup sweet potato puree
1/2 teaspoon nutmeg
Salt to taste
Freshly ground pepper to taste
2 tablespoons butter
2 tablespoons honey

Preheat oven to 350° F.
Peel onions and boil in salted water to cover for 15-20 minutes or until onions are tender but not falling apart. Cool slightly and take out centers. Save for soup. Mix sweet potato puree with remaining ingredients. Stuff centers of onions with potato. Put onions in baking dish with a quarter inch of water in bottom. Bake onions for 30 minutes.

PRALINE SWEET POTATOES
Serves 4-5

2 cups sweet potato puree
1 teaspoon salt
Freshly ground pepper to taste
¼ cup milk
1 egg
½ cup brown sugar, firmly
  packed
¼ cup melted butter or
  margarine
¼ cup dark corn syrup
½ cup ground pecans

Preheat oven to 350° F.

Beat together the sweet potato, salt, pepper, milk, and egg. Turn into greased 1-quart baking dish. Combine sugar, butter, and corn syrup and spread over potatoes. Sprinkle pecans over top. Bake for 25-30 minutes.

ONION AND POTATO BREAD
3 Loaves

1 package yeast
½ cup lukewarm water
3 tablespoons flour
½ cup onion puree
½ cup potato puree
2 tablespoons salt
2 cups water
9 cups flour (approximately)
2 teaspoons caraway seeds

Put yeast, lukewarm water, and 3 tablespoons flour in mixing bowl and let stand for 30 minutes. In large bowl put onion puree, potato puree, salt, and water. Add yeast, 7 cups flour, and caraway seeds. Beat well, mixing and adding flour until dough is no longer sticky. Turn out on floured board and knead until dough is smooth and elastic. Put dough into greased bowl and cover. Let rise in warm place until doubled in bulk. Punch down and shape into 3 round loaves. Put loaves into greased 10-inch round pans to rise. Cover and let rise until almost doubled. Preheat oven to 400° F. Brush tops of bread with water and bake for 1 hour until crusty. Cool on racks.

VEAL AND POTATO PIE
Serves 6

2 pounds lean veal cut into
  1-inch cubes
1 teaspoon salt
Freshly ground pepper to taste
Juice of ½ lemon
½ cup chicken bouillon
½ onion, sliced
Heavy cream, about ½ cup
6 tablespoons butter
½ pound mushrooms, sliced
4 tablespoons flour
2 tablespoons dry sherry
1 cup cooked diced carrots
1 cup cooked peas
1 cup cooked small white
  onions
½ cup hot milk
6 tablespoons butter
1 cup potato puree
Salt to taste
Freshly ground pepper to taste
1 egg yolk beaten with 1
  tablespoon cream

Preheat oven to 325° F.

Put veal in heavy casserole. Add salt, pepper, lemon juice, chicken bouillon, and onion. Cover tightly and braise in oven for 1½ hours. Remove and strain off accumulated liquid (about 1 cup). Measure and add cream to equal 1½ cups. Reserve. Heat butter and sauté mushrooms for 5 minutes. Sprinkle flour over mushrooms and cook, stirring, for 3-4 minutes. Add 1½ cups reserved liquid, bring to a boil and cook until thick and smooth. Add sherry and cook 2 minutes longer. Put veal, carrots, peas, and onions into buttered shallow baking dish (11 inches square and 2 inches deep). Pour mushroom sauce over all.

Heat milk with butter and when butter has melted beat into potato puree. Season with salt and pepper. Spread potato puree over top of baking dish, using a pastry tube if you wish. Brush with egg yolk. Bake at 400° F. for 30 minutes until golden and steaming.

Pumpkin

**Two pounds equals
2-plus cups puree.**

METHOD: Cut pumpkin in large pieces and put in baking pan. Pour 1 inch water in bottom. Cover with foil. Bake at 400° F. for 1 hour or until meat is very tender. Remove seeds and save for roasting. Remove meat and puree in blender, food processor or food mill. Can be frozen but do not can. (The experts do not recommend canning pumpkin at home because of its density.)

Pumpkins have changed. They are no longer just for jack-o'-lanterns and the meat is not pulpy and tough but sweet and tender, worth putting into a puree and preserving for future use.

Pumpkin soup is a colonial recipe and a very good starter for a winter supper. The only caution I have found in making this soup came from a French cookbook (we forget that pumpkin is also a European vegetable). It warns us not to keep the soup over 24 hours as the pumpkin may develop a sour taste. Good advice.

PUMPKIN MINCEMEAT TARTS
12 Tarts

12 2½-inch tart shells,
  unbaked
1 cup pumpkin puree
½ cup well-seasoned
  mincemeat
2 eggs
½ cup cream

Preheat oven to 425° F. and bake tart shells for 8 minutes.

Mix together the pumpkin puree, mincemeat, eggs, and cream. Fill each tart shell almost to the top. Reduce heat to 400° F. and bake for 20 minutes until puffed and firm. Serve with a rosette of whipped cream on each.

TART SHELLS
8 Shells

2 cups flour
½ cup ground walnuts
½ cup vegetable shortening or
  lard
¼ cup butter or margarine
1 teaspoon salt
1 egg yolk
2-3 tablespoons ice water

Put flour, nuts, shortenings, and salt into bowl of mixer. Beat quickly until just blended. Add yolk and beat, adding water until pastry is all together in a ball. It should clear the sides of the bowl and be pulled together, not dry and crumbly. Wrap in paper and chill. Roll out on floured board and cut into rounds with 3-inch cutter. Fit rounds into 2½-inch muffin cups. Prick bottoms with fork. Chill for 30 minutes. Fill and bake.

> Pumpkin and squash are interchangeable in many recipes and sometimes it is hard to tell one from the other. They both take very well to spices, either subtle or sharp. They both can be integral parts of recipes for breads, muffins, cakes, and pies. They both will serve as vegetables or desserts. New Englanders tend to flavor their pumpkin dishes with maple syrup and rum; Southerners lean toward molasses and bourbon. Either way, the combination is a pleasing one and we look forward to having pumpkin in some form around the holidays.

PUMPKIN PRALINE PIE
Serves 6

½ cup granulated sugar
½ cup brown sugar
½ teaspoon salt
1 tablespoon pumpkin pie
   spice
¼ cup dark molasses
2 cups pumpkin puree
3 eggs
1 cup whole milk
1 unbaked 9-inch pie shell
½ cup dark corn syrup
1 cup chopped pecans

Combine sugars and spices.

Beat together the molasses, pumpkin, eggs, and milk. Combine 2 mixtures, blending well. Turn into unbaked pie shell. Bake at 400° F. for 40 minute until set. Remove from oven and turn on broiler. Combine corn syrup and pecans and spread over top of pie. Broil until bubbly. Cool before cutting.

FROZEN PUMPKIN TORTE
Serves 6-8

1½ cups gingersnap crumbs
½ cup sugar
¼ cup melted butter or
   margarine
1 quart rum raisin ice cream
1 cup pumpkin puree
½ cup light brown sugar
2 tablespoons rum
½ teaspoon ground cloves
1 teaspoon ground cinnamon
½ cup heavy cream
½ cup chopped pecans

Mix together the crumbs, sugar, and melted butter. Press onto bottom and sides of 9-inch cake tin with removable bottom. Freeze for 10 minutes.

Soften ice cream and spread over crust. Freeze. Mix pumpkin with sugar, rum, and spices. Whip cream and fold in. Spread over ice cream and return to freezer. Freeze until firm.

Before serving sprinkle pecans over top. Run knife around edge of cake tin and remove to serving platter.

PUMPKIN NUT BARS
Approximately 24 bars

3 eggs, separated
½ cup granulated sugar
½ cup brown sugar
Grated rind of ½ orange
1 cup flour
1 teaspoon baking powder
½ teaspoon salt
1 cup pumpkin puree
1 cup nuts, chopped fine

Beat yolks until thick, adding sugars gradually. Add orange rind. Combine flour, baking powder, and salt. Beat whites until stiff but not dry. Stir one-third of whites into yolk mixture. Stir in pumpkin and nuts. Sift flour mixture and fold in. Fold in remaining beaten whites. Spread in 9x12-inch greased shallow pan. Bake at 350° F. for 30 minutes until puffed and firm. Cool on rack. Cut into bars.

JEAN HEWITT'S PUMPKIN FLAN
Serves 8

½ cup sugar
¾ cup light brown sugar
½ teaspoon cinnamon
½ teaspoon ground ginger
¼ teaspoon grated nutmeg
¼ teaspoon salt
1 cup pumpkin puree
1½ cups light cream
5 eggs, beaten
1 teaspoon vanilla
½ cup heavy cream, whipped

Place ½ cup sugar in heavy skillet and set over medium heat. Cook, shaking pan occasionally, until sugar turns a caramel color and is syrupy. Pour into 9-inch pie plate, turning to cover bottom.

In bowl combine brown sugar, cinnamon, ginger, nutmeg, salt, and pumpkin puree.

Mix together the light cream, eggs, and vanilla and blend into pumpkin mixture. Pour into pie plate. Set in pan of hot water and bake 1 hour at 350° F. or until knife inserted near middle comes out clean. Cool on rack. Chill.

To serve: loosen edges with knife and turn out onto serving plate. Decorate with whipped cream.

DATE GRAHAM TORTE

Serves 8-10

5 eggs, separated
½ cup sugar
1 cup graham cracker crumbs
1 teaspoon baking powder
½ teaspoon ginger
¼ teaspoon allspice
½ teaspoon nutmeg
½ pound dates, chopped
½ cup pumpkin puree
1 cup heavy cream

Beat egg whites with a pinch of salt until stiff. Without washing beater, beat yolks with sugar until thick. Combine crumbs, baking powder, add spices and mix with yolks. Stir in dates and pumpkin puree, blending well. Fold in whites. Turn into greased 8-inch spring form pan.

Bake at 325° F. for 40 minutes. Cool on rack. Remove sides of pan and when completely cool split cake into 2 layers. Fill and frost with whipped cream.

MOIST PUMPKIN GINGERBREAD

½ cup butter or margarine
½ cup brown sugar
½ cup maple syrup
1 cup pumpkin puree
2 cups flour
½ teaspoon salt
1 teaspoon ginger
½ teaspoon cinnamon
½ teaspoon allspice
1 teaspoon baking soda
2 eggs

Cream together until smooth the butter and sugar. Beat in syrup and pumpkin puree. Combine dry ingredients and stir in, mixing well. Beat in eggs. Turn into greased 9x9-inch pan. Bake for 30-35 minutes until cake tests done. Serve warm with whipped cream or hard sauce.

PUMPKIN CHARLOTTE
Serves 6

1 package plain gelatin
1 cup orange juice
1 cup sugar
1 package ladyfingers
1 cup pumpkin puree
1 teaspoon ground ginger
1 cup heavy cream, plus cream
    for topping
Chopped walnuts (optional)

Soak gelatin in ¼ cup orange juice.

Heat remaining juice with sugar, stirring until sugar is dissolved. Split ladyfingers and dip quickly into orange juice. Line bottom and sides of 1-quart soufflé dish.

Dissolve gelatin in warm orange juice. Stir in pumpkin and ginger. Refrigerate until syrupy.

Whip cream until stiff and fold into pumpkin mixture. Turn into lined soufflé dish. Chill until firm.

Before serving garnish top with whipped cream rosettes and chopped walnuts if desired.

PUMPKIN CHEESECAKE
Serves 12

8 ounces cream cheese
1 cup dry cottage cheese
2 eggs
½ cup pumpkin puree
½ teaspoon ground mace
1 cup sugar
1 teaspoon vanilla
1 tablespoon grated lemon
    rind
1½ cups dried whole wheat
    bread crumbs or graham
    cracker crumbs
¼ cup butter, melted

Beat together the cream cheese and cottage cheese. Beat in eggs. Add pumpkin puree, mace, ½ cup sugar, vanilla, and lemon rind. Mix well. Mix together the crumbs, butter, and ½ cup sugar. Press all but ¼ cup of crumb mixture onto bottom and sides of 8-inch spring form pan. Pour pumpkin mixture into crust. Sprinkle with remaining crumbs.

Bake at 325° F. for 45 minutes. Turn off heat and open oven door. Leave cake in oven for 1 hour. Remove and cool. Refrigerate for several hours before cutting.

PUMPKIN DOUGHNUTS
Approximately 24

1 cup sugar
1 cup pumpkin puree
4 tablespoons plain yogurt
2 tablespoons melted
  shortening
2 eggs
1 teaspoon baking soda
1 teaspoon baking powder
1 teaspoon cinnamon
½ teaspoon nutmeg
½ teaspoon salt
Approximately 4½ cups flour,
  half white and half whole
  wheat
Cinnamon sugar or powdered
  sugar
Fat for frying

In large bowl mix together the sugar, pumpkin, yogurt, shortening, and eggs. Combine dry ingredients and add, beating well. Chill. Roll out on floured board to ½-inch thickness. Cut with doughnut cutter.

Heat fat to 375° F. Drop doughnuts into fat and cook until deep brown, turning once. Drain on paper towels and dip into sugar.

PUMPKIN RING
Serves 6-8

4 eggs
4 cups pumpkin puree
1 cup milk
2 tablespoons grated onion
Grated rind of 1 orange
3 tablespoons orange liqueur
½ cup toasted bread crumbs
½ teaspoon ground ginger
½ teaspoon allspice

Preheat oven to 350° F.

Beat eggs into pumpkin puree. Add milk, blending well. Stir in remaining ingredients. Mix thoroughly. Turn into buttered 1½-quart ring mold. Set mold in pan of hot water and bake for 45-50 minutes until firm. Remove from water and let stand 10 minutes. Unmold onto serving platter and fill center with glazed onions.

PUMPKIN SOUP
Serves 6

6 tablespoons butter or
   margarine
2 leeks, chopped, white part
   only
2 stalks celery, chopped
1 onion, chopped
3 cups pumpkin puree
6 cups chicken bouillon
1 cup heavy cream
Salt to taste
Freshly ground pepper to taste
¼ cup bourbon whiskey

Heat butter in heavy saucepan and sauté leeks, celery, and onion until limp, about 8 minutes. Stir in pumpkin puree. Add chicken bouillon. Cover pan and simmer for 30 minutes. Stir in cream and season with salt and pepper. Add bourbon and bring to a boil. Serve immediately.

PUMPKIN RUM CUSTARD
Serves 6

3 eggs
¼ cup granulated sugar
1½ cups whole milk
½ cup cream
1 cup pumpkin puree
2 tablespoons rum
¼ cup brown sugar

Beat eggs with granulated sugar. Heat milk and cream to scalding and pour over eggs, beating constantly. Beat in pumpkin and rum. Sift brown sugar over bottom of 1-quart baking dish. Pour pumpkin mixture into dish. Set dish in pan of hot water. Bake for 45 minutes at 350° F. or until custard is set in center. Remove and cool before serving.

Spinach

One pound equals 1 cup puree.

METHOD: Wash and stem spinach leaves. Put in large pot. Sprinkle a little salt on leaves. Cover pot and put over high heat. As soon as leaves have wilted, about 5 minutes, remove and drain. Press liquid out of leaves. Chop fine, using knife or food processor. Blender tends to make too fine a puree. Can be frozen.

More greens — but they are so good for us! Spinach has really come of age since the days when it was served overcooked, limp, stringy, and still dripping its cooking water over the plate. It can take its place on the most sophisticated menu and even confirmed spinach haters will eat it happily. We now know that to be palatable it must be well drained, and to be thoroughly enjoyable it should be well seasoned.

Spinach has an affinity for nutmeg, garlic, onion, cheeses, tomato, butter, and cream. Start with the basic puree and add grated Parmesan, salt, pepper, and nutmeg. Fold this mixture into a soufflé or moisten with cream and stuff tomatoes. Add eggs and melted butter and make a spinach roll. Add mushrooms and bread crumbs and make fritters.

Take a cup of spinach puree and mix in some chopped parsley, a little garlic puree, salt, pepper, lemon juice, and 1 cup of oil and serve as a sauce over fish, pasta, or potato pancakes. Stuff eggs with spinach spiked with sharp cheese and Tabasco. Make spinach dumplings and serve with a cheese sauce or make our veal pie for an autumn picnic and take along bread, cheese, and wine for a glorious feast.

SPINACH SOUFFLÉ
Serves 4

2 tablespoons butter or
  margarine
2 tablespoons flour
½ cup chicken bouillon
½ cup milk
Salt to taste
Freshly ground pepper to taste
½ teaspoon nutmeg
1 cup spinach puree
5 egg yolks
6 egg whites
¼ cup finely grated Swiss
  cheese

Preheat oven to 350° F.

Heat butter in saucepan and add flour. Cook, stirring, for 3 minutes. Add bouillon and milk and cook, stirring, until thick and smooth. Remove from heat. Season. Stir in spinach puree. Add yolks one at a time, mixing well after each addition. Beat whites until stiff and fold into spinach mixture. Turn into 1½-quart greased soufflé dish. Sprinkle cheese over top. Bake for 30-35 minutes until firm and puffy. Serve immediately.

SPINACH FRITTERS
Serves 4

2 cups spinach puree, well
    drained
¼ cup flour
1 egg
½ teaspoon salt
½ teaspoon grated nutmeg
1 teaspoon grated onion
Freshly ground pepper to taste

Mix spinach with flour, egg, and seasonings. If mixture is too moist to handle easily, add more flour. Heat shortening in skillet. Make fritters 2-3 inches round and sauté until lightly browned on both sides. Serve with ham or bacon.

VEAL AND SPINACH PIE
Serves 6

1 pound ground veal
2 tablespoons grated onion
2 tablespoons cream
1 teaspoon dry mustard
½ teaspoon nutmeg
2 ripe tomatoes, peeled and
    sliced
1½ cups spinach puree
4 tablespoons grated Parmesan
    cheese
1 egg
¼ cup sour cream
Salt to taste
Freshly ground pepper to taste

Preheat oven to 350° F.

Mix veal with onion, cream, and seasonings. Spread over bottom of 9-inch pie dish. Arrange tomato slices over veal. Mix together the spinach puree, cheese, egg, and sour cream. Season to taste with salt and pepper. Spread over tomatoes. Bake for 40 minutes until top is firm. Serve at room temperature.

SPINACH ROLL
Serves 4

2 cups spinach puree, well
   drained
½ teaspoon grated nutmeg
1 tablespoon grated onion
½ teaspoon salt
Freshly ground pepper to taste
5 eggs, separated
6 tablespoons melted
   shortening

Preheat oven to 375° F.

Prepare pan: grease a 10x15-inch jelly roll pan. Cover with waxed paper, extending paper 1 inch over each end. Grease paper. Mix spinach with nutmeg, onion, salt, pepper, egg yolks, and melted shortening. Beat whites until stiff and fold in. Spread mixture evenly over waxed paper. Bake for 18 minutes. Turn out onto clean towel. Remove pan. Let roll stand for 5 minutes. Strip off paper. Roll up. Unroll and cool. Spread with creamed mushrooms or scrambled eggs and roll up. Reheat for 15 minutes in 325° F. oven. Slice and serve warm.

COLD SPINACH MOUSSE
Serves 6-8

2 packages unflavored gelatin
½ cup lemon juice
2 cups spinach puree
Salt to taste
Freshly ground pepper to taste
½ teaspoon nutmeg
1 cup mayonnaise
2 tablespoons grated onion
1 cup heavy cream

Soften gelatin in lemon juice. Set in pan of hot water until gelatin becomes liquid and clear. Put spinach puree in large bowl and season with salt, pepper, and nutmeg. Stir in mayonnaise and onion. Add gelatin. Whip cream until stiff and fold into spinach mixture. Turn into greased 6-cup ring mold. Chill for several hours until firm. Unmold onto serving platter and surround with thick tomato slices marinated in vinaigrette dressing and garnished with capers.

Winter Squash

One pound equals 2 cups puree.

METHOD: Cut squash in large pieces and put in baking pan. Pour 1 inch of water in bottom and cover with foil. Bake in 400° F. oven for 1 hour or until squash is very soft. Remove seeds and strings and scoop out meat. Put through food mill, or puree in blender or food processor. Can be frozen.

There are many varieties of winter squash, and they are all lovely to look at in the fall with their colors that range from deep green to bright red and orange. We can lump them all together when used as puree, although there are differences in taste and texture in the finished products.

Orange rind and ginger come to mind when thinking about appropriate seasonings for puddings, pancakes, or waffles; nutmeg, cinnamon, and allspice for cakes, cookies, and pies. These squashes go well with the fruits of the season such as apples and pears, and honey and maple syrup can be the sweeteners. Acorn squash puree is good when mixed with pear puree and piled back into the shells. Butternut makes lovely rolls, and Hubbard produces a pie that will give pumpkin a run for its money. (See how many people know the difference between the two.) If you have trouble keeping the winter squashes after the deep cold weather sets in, a puree is the way to save them and enjoy them all winter long.

PORK CHOPS WITH SQUASH STUFFING

Serves 6

1 cup cornbread crumbs
½ cup squash puree
Grated rind of 1 orange
8 prunes, chopped
½ teaspoon ground cardamon
Salt to taste
2 tablespoons grated onion
6 lean pork chops, 1 inch thick
Prepared mustard
Brown sugar
Bread crumbs
2 tablespoons shortening
½ cup cider
½ cup chicken broth
Orange slices

Mix together the cornbread crumbs, squash, orange rind, prunes, and cardamon. Season to taste with salt and onion. With sharp knife, cut a pocket in each chop and fill with stuffing. Close opening with skewer. Spread chops lightly with prepared mustard. Dip in brown sugar and coat with bread crumbs. Heat shortening in large skillet and brown chops on all sides.

Place chops in one layer in baking dish. Pour cider and broth over them. Cover and bake at 350° F. for 1 hour. If more liquid is needed while baking, to keep dish from drying, add cider and broth.

Garnish with orange slices.

BUTTERNUT SQUASH WAFFLES

Serves 4

2 cups all-purpose flour
4 teaspoons baking powder
¼ teaspoon salt
2 tablespoons brown sugar
2 eggs, separated
1 cup butternut squash puree
1½ cups buttermilk
½ cup melted butter or
    margarine

Combine dry ingredients in bowl. Beat in egg yolks, squash puree, buttermilk, and butter. Beat egg whites until stiff and fold in. Cook on waffle iron. Serve with ice cream and chopped pecans for dessert.

SQUASH SOUFFLÉ
Serves 6

2 tablespoons butter or
    margarine
2 tablespoons flour
½ cup chicken broth
½ cup milk
Salt to taste
Freshly ground pepper to taste
½ teaspoon cinnamon
¼ teaspoon ginger
¼ teaspoon nutmeg
1 cup squash puree
4 egg yolks
5 egg whites

Heat butter in saucepan. Stir in flour. Add liquids and bring to a boil, stirring. Cook until thick and smooth. Remove from heat. Stir in seasonings and squash. Blend well. Stir in egg yolks. Beat whites until stiff but not dry. Fold into squash mixture. Turn into 1½-quart soufflé dish and bake at 350° F. for 30-40 minutes until puffy and firm. Serve immediately with roast chicken or pork.

SQUASH CORN MUFFINS
12 Muffins

1 cup flour
½ cup stoneground cornmeal
⅓ cup sugar
2 teaspoons baking powder
½ teaspoon salt
4 tablespoons melted butter or
    margarine
1 egg
½ cup squash puree
½ cup plain yogurt

In large bowl combine flour, cornmeal, sugar, baking powder, and salt. Beat in butter, egg, and squash. Stir in yogurt and mix well.

Spoon batter into 12 2½-3-inch greased muffin cups. Bake at 375° F. for 15 minutes.

SQUASH CAKE
1 9x13-inch cake

2 cups flour
¼ teaspoon baking soda
2 teaspoons baking powder
½ teaspoon ground nutmeg
¼ teaspoon ground cloves
½ teaspoon cinnamon
½ teaspoon salt
¼ cup butter or margarine
1 cup maple syrup
2 eggs
¼ cup buttermilk
¾ cup winter squash puree
½ cup raisins
½ cup chopped walnuts

Preheat oven to 350° F.

Combine flour, baking soda, baking powder, and spices. Cream together the butter and syrup until smooth, then beat in eggs one at a time, mixing well. Beat in dry ingredients alternately with buttermilk and squash puree. Stir in raisins and nuts. Turn into greased and floured 9x13-inch baking pan. Bake for 30 minutes until cake tests done. Cool before serving.

SQUASH IN ORANGE CUPS
Serves 6

3 large oranges, cut in half
2 cups squash puree
2 tablespoons brown sugar
Salt to taste
1 teaspoon ginger
2 tablespoons butter or
    margarine

Juice oranges and remove pulp, leaving shells intact. Add enough juice to squash to make a soft mixture. Stir in sugar, salt, and ginger. Pile squash into orange shells and dot with butter. Bake at 350° F. until heated through, about 15 minutes. Serve with ham or turkey.

SQUASH OAT COOKIES
2 Dozen

¾ cup brown sugar
¾ cup honey
¾ cup butter or margarine
1 egg
2 cups flour
½ teaspoon salt
1 teaspoon cinnamon
½ teaspoon ground cardamom
½ teaspoon baking soda
2½ cups regular oats
½ cup squash puree
1 cup raisins

Cream sugar, honey, and butter until smooth. Beat in egg. Combine flour, salt, cinnamon, cardamom, and soda. Beat into creamed mixture. Add oats and mix well. Blend in squash puree. Stir in raisins.

Drop by tablespoons onto greased baking sheet. Bake at 375° F. for 10 minutes. Remove to rack and cool. Cookies will flatten and become crisp when cold.

NEW ENGLAND SQUASH PIE
Serves 6

⅓ cup sugar
⅓ cup brown sugar
½ teaspoon salt
½ teaspoon cinnamon
½ teaspoon nutmeg
¼ teaspoon ground cloves
¼ cup maple syrup
¼ cup rum
1½ cups squash puree
2 eggs
1 cup milk
1 unbaked 9-inch pie shell

Combine sugars and spices. Beat maple syrup, rum, and squash puree together. Beat in eggs and milk. Combine with dry ingredients. Turn into pie shell. Bake at 400° F. for 40 minutes until set. Cool slightly before cutting. Serve with sweetened rum-flavored whipped cream.

Yellow Squash

One pound equals 1 cup puree.

METHOD: Do not peel squash. Slice and put into saucepan with salted water about halfway up squash. Cover and bring to a boil. Cook until soft, about 10 minutes. Drain well. Puree through food mill or in blender or food processor. Drain again. Can be frozen.

I have the feeling that when zucchini came in, yellow or summer squash went out. Gardeners seem to plant more, eat more, and preserve more green than yellow squash these days. I know we do, and I think it's too bad because the old-fashioned yellow squash really has a lot to offer. Of course it needs good seasonings but what squash doesn't? It is pretty to look at, distinctly summery in appearance, and has a lightness of texture that is not found in the zucchini.

To get the best of squashes, combine the two in one dish. The yellow squash makes a delicious and unusual cold soup when pureed and cooked in chicken broth flavored with a small amount of garlic puree. Serve very cold with a spoonful of chopped cooked chicken and a dab of yogurt on top.

A soufflé-like pudding of squash puree, cracker crumbs, cottage cheese, and eggs is both pretty and palatable and goes very well with barbecued chicken. And just so you don't get the idea that zucchini is the *only* squash that can be made into a dessert, try yellow squash pie with lemon zest. It's a good old-fashioned vegetable that takes well to new ideas.

YELLOW SQUASH SOUFFLÉ

Serves 6

1 tablespoon butter or
   margarine
1 tablespoon flour
½ cup milk
Salt to taste
Freshly ground pepper to taste
1 teaspoon prepared mustard
½ cup mayonnaise
3 eggs, separated
1 cup yellow squash puree
1 cup grated cheese (mix two
   kinds, such as Parmesan and
   Swiss, Gouda and Cheddar,
   or Romano and Havarti)
2 tablespoons chopped parsley

Preheat oven to 350° F.

Heat butter and stir in flour. Cook, stirring, for 2 minutes. Add milk and cook, stirring, until thick. Remove from heat and add salt, pepper, and mustard. Stir in mayonnaise and egg yolks. Add squash and cheeses, mixing well. Beat egg whites until stiff and fold in. Turn into buttered 1½-quart soufflé dish. Bake for 30 minutes until puffed and golden. Sprinkle with chopped parsley and serve immediately.

YELLOW SQUASH PIE

Serves 6-8

2 cups squash puree
1 cup small curd cottage cheese
2 eggs
¼ cup medium dry sherry
¼ cup milk
¼ cup sugar
1 teaspoon ground nutmeg
Grated rind of ½ medium
   lemon
½ teaspoon salt
1 9-inch unbaked pie shell

Preheat oven to 375° F.

Beat together the squash puree and cottage cheese. Beat in eggs. Stir in sherry, milk, sugar, nutmeg, lemon rind, and salt. Pour into pie shell. Set pan on baking sheet and place on lower shelf of oven. Bake for 35-40 minutes until firm in the center and slightly puffed. Cool before serving.

Tomatoes

One pound equals 1 cup sauce.

METHOD: Wash tomatoes and cut in halves or quarters. Put in large non-aluminum pot over medium heat. Cook for 2-3 hours until tomatoes are very soft and most of the liquid has evaporated. Put through a food mill or Squeezo strainer. (Tomatoes can be put through Squeezo strainer before cooking.) If you wish a thicker sauce, return mixture to saucepan and cook longer.

Tomato sauce can be frozen or processed in boiling water bath. Add salt before processing.

Tomato sauce does not have to be part of an Italian meal. It is found with a variety of seasonings, in all Mediterranean foods. It combines well with all main course foods, salads, appetizers, and even dessert, as in our spicy tomato cake.

Eggs in various forms from omelets to soufflés benefit from the sharp flavor of tomato sauce; as does cheese in a fondu. Certain kinds of fish are traditionally served with tomato, such as salt cod in the Portuguese style, with lots of peppers, anchovies, and garlic. Halibut and swordfish take to tomato sauces, and shrimp is a natural.

SPAGHETTI AND MEATBALLS
Serves 8

2 pounds fresh chuck, ground
    twice
2 tablespoons grated Parmesan
    cheese
1½ teaspoons salt
Freshly ground pepper to taste
¼ cup breadcrumbs
1 cup muscat seeded raisins
1 tablespoon minced parsley
3 eggs
3 tablespoons butter
1 tablespoon oil
6 cups tomato puree
1 pound spaghetti

In a large bowl place chuck, cheese, salt, pepper, bread crumbs, raisins, parsley, and eggs, blending everything well. Form meatballs the size of golfballs, sauté them in the butter and oil in a large, deep saucepan or pot, turning so they are completely browned. Pour in the tomato puree and simmer, uncovered, stirring often, for 1 hour, or until sauce is smooth and thickened.

Cook spaghetti al dente; drain. It is the American custom to pour all the sauce over the pasta and toss so that it is heavily coated. The pasta is served on a large warm platter ringed with meatballs.

NEAPOLITAN PIZZAIOLA SAUCE

2 tablespoons olive oil
2 cloves garlic, minced
1 teaspoon dried oregano or 1
    tablespoon chopped
    fresh basil or 2 tablespoons
    chopped parsley
Salt to taste
Freshly ground pepper to taste
3 cups tomato puree

A light tomato sauce usually served on steaks.

Heat oil and sauté garlic for 2 minutes. Add remaining ingredients and cook over medium high heat for 10 minutes.

CHEESE DREAMS

½ pound cheddar cheese
4 slices bacon
1 small onion
Tomato puree
1 loaf unsliced white bread

Put cheese, bacon, and onion through meat grinder. Mix together with tomato puree to make a spreadable mixture, fairly soft.

Cut crusts off loaf of bread and slice the long way into 5 slices. Flatten slices with rolling pin and spread with cheese mixture. Roll up the long way as for a jelly roll. Wrap in plastic wrap and refrigerate. Cut into ½-inch slices and place on baking sheets. Bake at 450° F. for 10 minutes until golden and toasted.

SHRIMP IN SPICY ORANGE SAUCE
Serves 4

3 tablespoons vegetable oil
4 large cloves garlic, peeled
2 cups tomato puree
¾ cup orange marmalade
Juice of ½ lemon
1 tablespoon chopped fresh
   ginger root
Salt to taste
1½ pounds shelled shrimp

Heat oil in heavy saucepan or skillet and add garlic. Cook over medium heat for 10 minutes until golden, turning frequently. Do not burn.

Add tomato puree and cook over medium heat for 10 minutes. Stir in all remaining ingredients except shrimp and cook for 15-20 minutes, until slightly thickened.

Add shrimp and cook for 5-7 minutes until shrimp are pink and firm. Serve over rice.

CURRIED TOMATOES
Serves 6

6 ripe tomatoes, peeled
1 cup tomato puree
2 teaspoons curry powder or to taste
2 tablespoons currant jelly
¼ cup grated sharp cheddar cheese
3 tablespoons bread crumbs
6 crisp bacon slices

Place tomatoes in greased baking dish.

In saucepan combine tomato puree, curry powder, and jelly. Stir over medium heat for 5 minutes or until well blended. Pour over tomatoes. Sprinkle with cheese and crumbs. Bake at 425° F. for 15 minutes. Garnish with bacon.

TOMATO BARLEY PILAF
Serves 6

6 tablespoon butter or margarine
¼ pound fresh mushrooms, sliced
1 medium onion, chopped
1 cup medium pearl barley
2 cups chicken bouillon
½ cup small curd cottage cheese
½ cup plain yogurt
½ cup tomato sauce
Salt to taste
Freshly ground pepper to taste
2 tablespoons chopped parsley

Preheat oven to 350° F.

Heat 4 tablespoons butter in large skillet. Quickly sauté mushrooms over high heat, stirring until just coated with butter. They should be firm. Remove mushrooms with a slotted spoon and reserve. Add remaining butter and onion to skillet. Sauté onion until just limp. Add barley and cook, stirring until golden on all sides. Add chicken bouillon. Cover and reduce heat to low. Cook until barley is tender, about 30 minutes. Stir in mushrooms, cottage cheese, yogurt, and tomato sauce. Season to taste. Turn into buttered 1½-quart baking dish and bake for one hour. Garnish with parsley.

TOMATO CLAM BROTH
Serves 4

2 tablespoons butter or
  margarine
1 carrot, chopped
1 stalk celery, chopped
½ green pepper, diced
1 small onion, chopped
2 cups tomato puree
2 cups clam broth
1 cup white wine
Salt and pepper to taste
Chopped parsley

Heat butter in saucepan and sauté carrot, celery, pepper, and onion until soft. Add tomato puree and clam broth. Bring to a boil. Reduce heat and simmer, covered, for 30 minutes. Strain. Return broth to pan and add wine, salt and pepper. Simmer for 10 minutes. Serve hot garnished with parsley.

TOMATO AND ONION SOUP
Serves 4

3 tablespoons butter
2 tablespoons oil
3 large sweet onions, thinly
  sliced
2 cups tomato puree
4 cups chicken broth or water
1 teaspoon sugar
½ teaspoon grated nutmeg
Salt to taste
8 slices French bread fried in
  oil
½ cup grated Gruyère cheese

Heat butter and oil in large saucepan. Add onions and stir to coat thoroughly.

Reduce heat to simmer and cover pan. Cook over very low heat for 30-40 minutes until onions are very soft. Add tomato puree, broth, and seasonings. Bring to a boil. Place 2 slices bread in each soup bowl and sprinkle with half of cheese. Pour soup over bread and sprinkle with remaining cheese. Serve immediately.

CHICKEN LIVER SAUCE

¼ **pound bacon, minced**
1 **small onion, minced**
¼ **cup minced parsley**
½ **pound chicken livers,**
  quartered
¼ **pound mushrooms, thinly**
  sliced
¼ **cup Marsala wine**
½ **cup tomato puree**
Salt and pepper to taste
½ **teaspoon ground sage**

Chop together the bacon, onion, and parsley to make a paste. Put into deep skillet and cook, stirring, for 5 minutes. Add chicken livers and mushrooms. Cook over medium heat until livers are browned. Add remaining ingredients and cook for 10 minutes. Serve over spaghetti.

SICILIAN SWEET AND SOUR SAUCE

2 **tablespoons vegetable oil**
¼ **cup minced onion**
¼ **cup chopped parsley**
2 **tablespoons chopped basil**
2 **cups tomato puree**
Salt to taste
Freshly ground pepper to taste
1-**inch cinnamon stick**
1 **teaspoon sugar**
1 **tablespoon wine vinegar**

Heat oil and sauté onion, parsley, and basil until soft. Add tomato, salt, pepper, and cinnamon. Cook over low heat, stirring occasionally, until slightly thickened. Add sugar dissolved in vinegar. Simmer 5 minutes. Remove cinnamon stick and serve with broiled fish.

PAELLA VALENCIANA
Serves 4-5

⅓ cup vegetable oil
1 3-pound frying chicken, cut
   into serving pieces
1 large onion, chopped
1 clove garlic, chopped
1 cup rice (not minute rice)
¼ teaspoon saffron
Salt to taste
Pepper to taste
Dash of Tabasco
½ cup tomato puree
2 cups chicken stock or stock
   and water mixed
12 unshelled cherrystone
   clams
½ pound shrimp, shelled and
   cleaned
1 pound hot or sweet sausage,
   cooked and sliced
1 cup peas
Parsley
Pimiento strips

Heat oil and brown chicken on all sides. Remove. Add onion and garlic and sauté until soft. Add rice and cook until it turns yellow. Season with saffron, salt, and pepper. Add Tabasco. Add tomato puree, stock, and chicken. Cover and cook until rice is tender, about 20 minutes. Add unshelled clams, shrimp, and sausages. Continue cooking until chicken is tender and shrimp are cooked. Add peas and cook 5 minutes.

Garnish with parsley and pimiento strips.

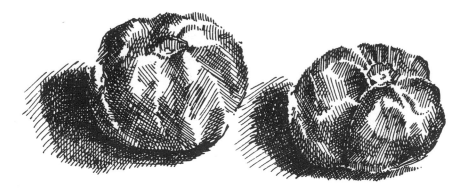

TOMATOES WITH TOMATO SOUFFLÉ
Serves 4

4 large tomatoes
1½ tablespoons butter
2 teaspoons grated onion
1½ tablespoons flour
½ teaspoon curry powder, or
   to taste
½ cup milk
2 egg yolks
Salt and pepper to taste
1 cup tomato puree
3 egg whites

Scoop out insides of tomatoes and turn upside down to drain. Heat butter and add grated onion. Cook for 1 minute. Add flour and curry powder and mix well. Add milk and cook, stirring, until sauce is thick and smooth. Remove from heat and add egg yolks. Season. Add tomato puree. Beat whites until stiff and fold in. Fill tomato shells and place them in a shallow dish. Bake at 375° F. for 25-30 minutes until set and puffy. Serve immediately with green salad and corn muffins.

BAKED EGG CASSEROLE
Serves 4

1 tablespoon oil
2 tablespoons butter or
   margarine
½ green pepper, chopped fine
1 small onion, chopped fine
1 stalk celery, chopped
3 tablespoons flour
1 teaspoon curry powder
½ cup milk
1 cup tomato puree
Salt and freshly ground
   pepper to taste
6 hardcooked eggs, sliced
½ cup buttered bread crumbs

Heat oil and butter in skillet. Add pepper, onion, and celery, and sauté until vegetables are soft. Stir in flour and curry powder and cook for 3 minutes. Stir in milk and tomato puree and cook until thickened and smooth. Season. Add eggs. Turn into buttered baking dish. Sprinkle top with crumbs. Bake at 350° F. for 20 minutes.

TOMATO FONDU
About 2 cups

1 tablespoon butter
2 tablespoons minced onion
½ cup finely chopped
   prosciutto ham
1 cup tomato puree
¼ teaspoon garlic puree
½ teaspoon oregano
Salt to taste
Freshly ground pepper to taste
½ teaspoon sugar
1 egg
¼ cup grated Romano cheese

Heat butter and sauté onion for 2-3 minutes. Stir in ham, tomato puree, garlic puree, oregano, salt, pepper, and sugar. Cook over medium heat for five minutes until well blended. Stir in egg and Romano cheese and cook 5 minutes longer, stirring, until thickened. Serve hot in a chafing dish surrounded with bread sticks or thin slices of Italian bread.

SARDINES IN TOMATO WINE SAUCE
Serves 4

2 tablespoons butter or
   margarine
1 tablespoon shallots, chopped
1 tablespoon chopped onion
1 garlic clove, minced
½ cup red wine
½ cup tomato puree
2 cans Portuguese sardines in
   oil
1 tablespoon snipped dill
   weed
Salt and pepper to taste

Heat butter and sauté shallots, onion, and garlic until soft. Add wine and tomato puree. Bring to a boil and simmer for 10 minutes. Drain sardines and place in one layer in shallow dish. Pour hot mixture over sardines and sprinkle with dill. Let stand at room temperature for 1 hour.

Spread 4 pieces of buttered rye toast lightly with mustard. Place sardines on toast and cover with sauce. Serve for lunch with a green salad.

TURKISH MEATBALLS IN TOMATO SAUCE

Serves 4

½ cup cider
2 thick slices whole wheat
  bread
1 pound lean ground lamb
1 medium onion, chopped fine
2 tablespoons chopped parsley
1 teaspoon paprika
Salt to taste
2 eggs
½ cup flour
2 tablespoons butter
1 tablespoon oil
2 cups tomato puree

Preheat oven to 325° F.

Heat ¼ cup cider and soak bread slices in it for 3 minutes. Squeeze bread dry. In mixing bowl put lamb, onion, parsley, paprika, salt, eggs, and bread. With hands mix all together until well blended. Do not be afraid of overworking the meat. Shape meat into balls, about 1½ inches in diameter. Dust balls lightly with flour. Heat butter and oil in skillet and brown meatballs on all sides. Remove meatballs to baking dish. Add tomato puree and remaining cider to skillet. Bring to a boil, stirring, and pour over meatballs. Bake for 30 minutes. Serve with rice pilaf.

SPICY LENTILS

Serves 4

1 cup lentils
2 tablespoons oil
1 clove garlic, minced
1 medium onion, chopped fine
1 cup tomato puree
1 teaspoon ground cumin
Salt and freshly ground
  pepper to taste
1 tablespoon vinegar
2 tablespoons chopped parsley
2 tablespoons chopped chives

Cook lentils in salted water until just tender. Drain. In large skillet heat oil and add garlic and onion. Sauté until soft. Stir in tomato puree, cumin, salt, and pepper. Add lentils and cook for 10 minutes.

Turn into serving dish and stir in vinegar. Sprinkle with parsley and chives and let stand 2 hours.

Serve at room temperature.

CHICKEN IN SPICY TOMATO SAUCE

Serves 4-6

2 cups tomato puree
½ orange, sliced thin and
  seeded
1 lemon, sliced thin and
  seeded
2 cups sugar
1 stick cinnamon
2 teaspoons whole cloves
1 chicken, cut into serving
  pieces
2 tablespoons butter
1 tablespoon vegetable oil
Salt and freshly ground
  pepper to taste

Put tomato puree, orange slices, lemon slices, sugar, and spices into large deep saucepan. (Contain cinnamon and cloves in cheesecloth bag.) Boil over medium heat, stirring frequently, until thick. This could take up to an hour depending on moisture in tomatoes. Heat butter and oil in skillet. Rub salt and pepper into chicken. Sauté chicken until browned on all sides. Remove to baking dish. Spoon sauce over chicken pieces. Cover with foil and bake in 350° F. oven for 40 minutes. Serve with rice and corn fritters.

STOFADO

Serves 6

2 whole chicken breasts, split
4 chicken thighs
4 tablespoons vegetable oil
Salt and pepper to taste
2 pounds white onions
2 cups tomato puree
1 bay leaf
1 teaspoon thyme
3 sprigs parsley
5 garlic cloves, peeled
½ cup chopped walnuts
¼ cup crumbled Feta cheese

Place chicken pieces skin side up on baking sheet. Brush with oil. Broil about 4 inches away from heat until golden. Turn and brush with oil. Broil undersides until golden. Place in deep casserole. Sprinkle with salt and pepper. Put onions into saucepan of cold water and bring to a boil. Boil for 5 minutes. Drain. Remove skins and with point of knife make an X in root ends of onions. Add to casserole. Pour tomato puree over all. Bury herbs and garlic cloves in sauce. Cover dish and bake at 275° F. for 4 hours. Before serving sprinkle with walnuts and cheese.

98

ARROZ CON POLLO

Serves 4-5

¼ cup vegetable oil
1 3-pound frying chicken cut up
1 onion, chopped
1 green pepper, chopped
1 clove garlic, minced
½ cup rice (not minute rice)
2 cups tomato puree
1 cup chicken broth
½ teaspoon saffron
Salt to taste
Freshly ground pepper to taste
1 box frozen peas
½ cup sliced olives, green or black
1 2-ounce jar pimiento pieces

Heat 2 tablespoons oil in large skillet. Sauté chicken pieces until golden. Remove to deep baking dish. Add remaining oil and sauté onion, pepper, and garlic until soft. Add rice and sauté, stirring, for 3 minutes. Add tomato puree, broth, saffron, salt, and pepper and bring to a boil. Pour over chicken.

Bake at 350° F. for 40 minutes. Add peas and olives and continue cooking for 10 minutes. Before serving garnish with pimientos and chopped parsley.

SHRIMP MOUSSE

1 package plain gelatin
¼ cup cold water
1 cup tomato puree
1 8-ounce package cream cheese
1 cup mayonnaise
½ cup chopped celery
½ cup chopped onion
½ cup chopped green pepper
1 cup cooked shrimp, cut up
Salt and pepper to taste

Soak gelatin in ¼ cup cold water. Heat tomato puree and dissolve gelatin in it. Beat cream cheese and mayonnaise together until creamy. Stir in tomato mixture, chopped vegetables, and shrimp. Season. Turn into 1½-quart oiled mold. Refrigerate for several hours. Turn out and surround with crackers or melba toast.

TOMATO PASTRY

2 eggs
7 tablespoons salad or olive oil
1 teaspoon salt
1 teaspoon sugar
1 clove garlic, mashed
½ cup tomato sauce
3 tablespoons grated Parmesan
  or Romano cheese
3 cups flour
2 teaspoons baking powder
Hot dogs or sausages

Preheat oven to 375° F.

Beat eggs in large bowl. Beat in 5 tablespoons oil. Stir in salt, sugar, garlic, tomato sauce, and cheese. Combine flour and baking powder and mix in, blending well. Dough should be easy to handle and not sticky. Turn out onto lightly floured board and knead in remaining 2 tablespoons oil. Shape dough around hot dogs (enough for 12) or cooked and drained sausages, enclosing meat entirely. Put on lightly greased baking sheet and bake for 10-15 minutes until golden. This dough can also be folded around meat or chicken fillings or small cocktail frankfurters.

CHILI PASTA ROLLS
Serves 6

3 tablespoons butter
2 cups cooked pasta of the
  acini type (small granules)
3 tablespoons whipping cream
1 teaspoon chili powder
Salt and pepper to taste
3 tablespoons chopped parsley
6 eggs
Chicken filling (see next
  recipe)
1½ cups tomato puree,
  seasoned with salt and
  pepper
¼ cup grated cheddar cheese

Grease 10x15-inch jelly roll pan. Cover with waxed paper leaving 1-inch surplus at either end. Grease paper. Heat butter in skillet and sauté cooked pasta for 3 minutes. Add cream. Remove from heat and stir in chili powder, salt, pepper, and parsley. Turn into large bowl and mix in eggs, blending well. Turn mixture into prepared pan. Bake at 350° F. for 20 minutes until firm and golden. Turn out onto clean towel. Remove pan. Strip off waxed paper.

Cut roll down the middle lengthwise and 3 times across making 8 pieces. Roll up each piece. Unroll and fill with chicken filling. Place filled rolls in buttered ovenproof dish, cover with tomato puree and sprinkle with grated cheese.

Reheat and serve with green salad, Italian bread and cheese.

CHICKEN FILLING

½ cup cooked chicken,
  chopped fine
½ cup cooked hot sausage,
  chopped fine
1 tablespoon butter
2 tablespoons minced onion
2 tablespoons flour
½ cup chicken bouillon
2 tablespoons whipping cream
Salt and pepper

In bowl mix together the chicken and sausage. Heat butter and sauté onion for 5 minutes. Stir in flour and cook, stirring, for 2 minutes. Add bouillon and cook, stirring, until thick and smooth. Add cream. Bring to a boil. Remove from heat and season to taste. Blend into chicken mixture. Fill each pasta roll.

CHICKEN CACCIATORA
Serves 4

1 3-pound frying chicken cut
  into pieces
½ cup flour
1 teaspoon salt
1 teaspoon paprika
¼ cup oil
2 garlic cloves, minced
1 small onion, chopped
1 carrot, chopped
1 stalk celery, chopped
3 sprigs parsley, chopped
1 bay leaf
2 cups tomato puree
¼ cup dry white wine

Dredge chicken with flour mixed with salt and paprika. Heat oil and brown chicken on all sides. Remove. Sauté garlic, onion, carrot, and celery until soft. Add parsley, bay leaf, and tomato puree. Bring to a boil. Add chicken and wine and reduce heat. Simmer, covered, for 30 minutes. Serve with pasta.

TOMATO RISOTTO CROQUETTES
12 Croquettes

2 tablespoons butter or
   margarine
1 tablespoon chopped shallot
½ cup regular long grain rice
½ cup chicken broth
1 cup tomato puree
½ teaspoon salt
⅓ cup grated Parmesan cheese
2 eggs, beaten
1 cup bread crumbs
Oil for deep frying

Heat butter in saucepan and sauté shallot and rice for 2-3 minutes, stirring.

Heat broth and tomato puree and add to rice. Add salt. Cover pan and reduce heat to low boil. Cook for 15-20 minutes until rice is tender and liquid is absorbed. Stir in Parmesan. Pack mixture into 1½-inch muffin tins. Cover with plastic wrap and chill 2-3 hours.

Heat oil to 375° F. Coat croquettes with beaten egg and crumbs. Fry until golden on all sides.

Serve with a small amount of pesto sauce on each croquette.

MEAT LOAF MARIA LUISA
Serves 4

¼ cup milk
½ cup tomato puree
2 slices bread, crusts removed
1½ pounds lean ground beef
2 tablespoons minced onion
1 clove garlic, minced
1 tablespoon Worcestershire
   sauce
2 eggs
Salt to taste
Freshly ground pepper to taste
½ cup grated Parmesan cheese
1 teaspoon oregano
½ teaspoon basil
1 cup ricotta cheese

In small saucepan heat together the milk and ¼ cup tomato puree. Add bread slices and let stand until well soaked.

In a large bowl mix together beef, onion, garlic, Worcestershire, eggs, and bread mixture. Season with salt and pepper. Mix in ¼ cup Parmesan. Mix oregano and basil with ricotta.

Put a third of the meat mixture into oiled baking dish and shape into a rectangle. Spread with half of ricotta. Pat another third of the meat over ricotta and top with remaining ricotta. Put the remaining third of the meat over top and cover with remaining ¼ cup tomato sauce. Sprinkle ¼ cup Parmesan over all. Bake at 350° F. for 45 minutes.

HUNGARIAN GOULASH

Serves 6

2 pounds lean beef chuck
Seasoned flour (1 teaspoon
   salt, ½ teaspoon pepper to 1
   cup flour)
3 tablespoons vegetable oil
2 large onions
1 clove garlic
1 cup tomato puree
1 cup red wine
1 bay leaf
1 teaspoon thyme
3 sprigs parsley
Salt and freshly ground
   pepper to taste
1 tablespoon Hungarian
   paprika

Cut beef into cubes. Dredge in seasoned flour. Heat oil in skillet and brown beef on all sides. Remove. Add onions and garlic to skillet and brown lightly. Stir in tomato puree, wine, herbs, and seasonings (but not paprika). Bring to a boil. Reduce heat and return meat to pan. Cover and simmer for 2 hours until meat is very tender. Stir in paprika and simmer 15 minutes longer. Serve with boiled potatoes or caraway noodles.

SWISS STEAK

Serves 4

¼ cup flour
Salt and pepper to taste
2 pounds round steak cut 1
   inch thick
2 tablespoons vegetable oil
1 large onion, sliced
1 cup tomato puree
1 cup beef bouillon
¼ cup steak sauce
2 tablespoons mustard
1 tablespoon sugar

Combine flour, salt, and pepper and rub or pound into meat on both sides. Heat oil and brown meat. Remove. Add more oil to skillet if necessary and wilt onion. Add tomato puree, bouillon, steak sauce, mustard, and sugar. Bring to a boil and cook until well blended. Return meat to skillet. Cover and simmer for 2-3 hours until meat is very tender.

Serve with mashed potatoes and a green vegetable.

CIOPPINO
Serves 6

½ cup vegetable oil
½ cup each chopped onions
    and scallions
1 green pepper, chopped
2 garlic cloves, chopped
3 cups tomato puree
2 cups red wine
1 bay leaf
Salt and pepper to taste
2 pounds firm white fish cut in
    large pieces
1 cooked lobster or Dungeness
    crab cut in pieces
1 pound shrimp, shelled
1 pint clams or mussels

In deep heavy saucepan heat oil. Add onions, scallions, green pepper, and garlic and cook until soft. Add tomato puree and red wine. Add bay leaf and salt and pepper to taste. Bring to a boil and simmer for 10 minutes. Add fish, lobster or crab, and shrimp. Cook 15 minutes. Add clams or mussels and cook for 5 minutes.

Serve very hot in deep bowls with plenty of French bread and red wine.

FROZEN TOMATO SALAD
Serves 6

1 8-ounce package cream
    cheese
1½ cups mayonnaise (not
    salad dressing)
1 onion, grated
Juice of ½ lemon
1 teaspoon salt
Dash of Tabasco
3 cups tomato puree
1½ packages plain gelatin
1 cup finely chopped celery

Soften cream cheese and beat in mayonnaise, onion, and seasonings. Soften gelatin in ¼ cup tomato puree. Dissolve by placing cup in hot water until gelatin is liquid. Stir into remaining tomato puree and combine with cheese mixture. Fold in celery. Turn into 6-cup ring mold. Freeze. Remove to refrigerator 1 hour before serving. Turn out and garnish with cucumbers and greens. Serve with tuna or chicken salad.

104

NEAPOLITAN TART
Serves 6

1 cup tomato puree
1 clove garlic, mashed and
   chopped
½ teaspoon oregano
1 teaspoon basil
Salt and freshly ground
   pepper to taste
1 cup ricotta cheese
3 eggs
Whole wheat pastry for one
   8-inch crust
½ cup grated Parmesan cheese

Combine tomato puree with garlic, oregano, basil, salt, and pepper. Beat eggs with ricotta. Combine two mixtures, blending well. Pour into pastry-lined pie shell and sprinkle with Parmesan cheese.

Set pie pan on baking sheet and bake at 350° F. for 30 minutes until puffed and firm.

Let stand 10 minutes before cutting.

RED AND WHITE ASPIC
Serves 6

2 packages unflavored gelatin
3 cups tomato puree
2 tablespoons sugar
2 tablespoons lemon juice
1 teaspoon Worcestershire
Dash of Tabasco
Salt to taste

Dissolve gelatin in ½ cup puree. Heat remaining puree with sugar, lemon juice, Worcestershire, Tabasco, and salt. Stir gelatin mixture into hot liquid. Turn into rinsed 1½-quart ring mold. Chill until firm.

1 package unflavored gelatin
¼ cup cold water
1 cup chicken broth with fat
   removed
1 8-ounce package cream
   cheese
2 tablespoons mayonnaise

Dissolve gelatin in cold water. Heat broth and stir gelatin into it. Add cream cheese and stir over medium heat until mixture is creamy and well blended. Cool. Stir in mayonnaise. Pour over tomato aspic and chill until firm. Unmold and serve with chicken salad, garnished with avocado.

TOMATO GOUGERE
Serves 6

4 tablespoons butter or
  margarine
½ cup tomato puree
½ cup water
1 teaspoon salt
Freshly ground pepper to taste
½ teaspoon oregano
2 drops Tabasco
1 cup flour
4 eggs
¼ cup finely ground ham
½ cup grated Parmesan cheese
1 egg yolk

Put butter, tomato, water, and seasonings into saucepan. Bring to a boil. When boiling hard, add flour and stir rapidly with wooden spoon for 2 minutes over heat until dough forms a ball. Remove from heat.

Beat in eggs, one at a time. Be sure each egg is thoroughly incorporated into batter before adding the next one. Batter should be fairly stiff and shiny. Beat in ham and ¼ cup cheese.

With spoon, drop large puffs of dough onto greased baking sheet to form a wreath of dough. Brush with beaten egg yolk and sprinkle with remaining cheese. Bake at 375° F. for 40-45 minutes until puffed and firm.

Serve immediately with a green salad for lunch or supper.

CANELLONI FOR FORTY

8 boxes frozen spinach
12 whole chicken breasts,
  1-pound each
1½ cups butter or margarine
1½ cups flour
6 cups chicken broth
6 cups milk
1-2 cups cream
Salt, pepper, nutmeg, mustard
115 crepes
4-5 cups tomato puree
1-1½ cups grated Parmesan
  cheese

Cook spinach. Drain and squeeze dry and chop fine. Poach chicken breasts until just tender. Remove meat from bones and chop fine. Combine spinach and chicken.

Heat butter and flour in large saucepan and stir, cooking until bubbly and golden. Add broth and milk and cook, stirring, until thick and smooth. Add cream gradually until sauce is consistency of heavy cream. Season to taste with salt, pepper, nutmeg, and mustard. Add enough sauce to chicken mixture to moisten.

Fill each crepe with about 3 tablespoons chicken mixture. Roll up and put into shallow baking dishes in which you have spread a small amount of tomato puree. Pour remaining sauce over crepes. Pour remaining tomato puree over sauce. Sprinkle with Parmesan.

Heat in 350° F. oven for 20 minutes until sauce is bubbling.

Serve with a green salad and French bread.

MANHATTAN CLAM PIE
Serves 4

4 slices bacon
1 onion, chopped
½ green pepper, chopped
2 stalks celery, chopped
1 potato, peeled and diced
1 egg
½ cup tomato puree
2 tablespoons chopped parsley
1 tablespoon snipped dill
   weed
Salt to taste
Freshly ground pepper to taste
2 drops Tabasco
2 9-ounce cans clams or 1 pint
   clams, drained
Pastry for top crust

Fry bacon until cooked but soft. Drain and chop. In bacon fat sauté onion, pepper, celery, and potato until soft.

Beat together the egg, tomato puree, and seasonings. Into 8-inch pie pan put half the sautéed vegetables. Cover with clams and bacon. Top with remaining vegetables. Pour sauce over all.

Roll out pastry and fit over pie, crimping edges. Make vents in top with knife point.

Bake at 400° F. for 25-30 minutes until browned.

Put some tomato sauce in your salad dressing, or combine it with cucumbers in soup. Use tomato sauce as the liquid for a pilaf, or in biscuits, or even breadsticks. By varying the seasonings and spices, possibly making it sweet instead of hot, you can use up most of your winter's supply by early spring. Next year you'll make more.

SPICY TOMATO NUT CAKE
1 9-inch tube cake

½ cup butter or margarine
1½ cups granulated sugar
1 cup brown sugar
3 cups unbleached flour
1 cup whole wheat pastry flour
2½ teaspoons baking soda
2 teaspoons cinnamon
1½ teaspoons salt
1 teaspoon nutmeg
½ teaspoon allspice
2½ cups tomato puree
2 teaspoons vanilla
1 cup chopped walnuts

Preheat oven to 350° F.

Cream butter and sugars until light. Combine dry ingredients. Add dry ingredients alternately to creamed mixture with tomato puree. Stir in vanilla and nuts. Turn into well greased and floured 9-inch tube pan. Bake for 1 hour and 10 minutes or until cake tests done in center. Cool cake in pan on rack for 10 minutes. Run knife around edge and turn out onto rack.

Zucchini

One pound equals 1½ cups puree.

METHOD: Because zucchini has so much liquid in it, I have found the best method for preserving it in a puree form is to grate or shred it very fine, sprinkle with salt and drain in a colander, squeeze grated zucchini with your hands, pressing out excess liquid, then sauté briefly in a very small amount of oil to get rid of the last bit of moisture. Now it can be used or frozen, for later use.

This will give you manageable amounts of non-watery zucchini to use all winter in soups with celery and onion, in tomato or white wine sauce for pasta, or in a light, creamy custard made like a quiche with eggs, cream, and cheese (perhaps some bacon or ham) and baked in a quiche dish without the crust.

We have found that the slight texture of grated zucchini even does a lot for cakes and cookies — try our oat bars.

When you have eaten all the nice tiny zucchini in your garden, grate up the big ones. They will be just as tender if used immediately, and you'll be glad you did when you start to make our leftover turkey casserole — page 112, two days after Christmas.

ZUCCHINI CRUSTLESS QUICHE
Serves 4-5

3 eggs
1 cup milk
½ cup sour cream
1 cup zucchini puree
1 teaspoon dill
½ teaspoon grated nutmeg
Salt to taste
Freshly ground pepper to taste
½ cup grated Swiss cheese
¼ cup ground ham (optional)
1 tablespoon butter or
  margarine

Preheat oven to 350° F.

Beat together the eggs and milk. Stir in sour cream and zucchini, blending well. Add seasonings. Sprinkle cheese over bottom of 9-inch pie pan. If using ham, sprinkle over cheese. Pour zucchini mixture over all. Dot with butter. Bake for 30 minutes until firm and puffy. Let stand 10 minutes before serving.

ZUCCHINI POTATO FRITTERS
Serves 4

2 cups grated zucchini
1 cup potato puree
2 tablespoons grated onion
½ teaspoon garlic puree
1 tablespoon chopped parsley
Salt to taste
Freshly ground pepper to taste
½ cup grated Parmesan cheese
1 egg
¼ cup flour
3 tablespoons vegetable oil
2 tablespoons butter

Mix together until well blended the zucchini, potato, onion, garlic, parsley, salt, pepper, cheese, and egg. Mixture should form into patties easily. If too dry, add some oil. Shape into patties, and dust with flour. Heat oil and butter over medium high heat in large skillet. Fry fritters until crisp and golden. Serve with baked fish or chicken a la king.

ZUCCHINI BAKED EGGS

Serves 1-2

1 tablespoon butter or
  margarine
1 cup grated zucchini, peeled
  or not
½ cup sour cream
1 tablespoon chopped parsley
2 teaspoons chopped chives
Salt and freshly ground
  pepper to taste
2 eggs
2 tablespoons finely grated
  Swiss cheese

Heat butter in medium-sized skillet. Add zucchini and cook, stirring, for 2-3 minutes. Stir in sour cream, parsley, chives, salt, and pepper. When mixture is heated through, make two indentations with the back of a spoon and break in the eggs. Sprinkle with cheese. Cover pan and turn heat down to simmer. Cook until whites are firm and yolks opaque, about 8-10 minutes.

ZUCCHINI CUSTARDS

Serves 8

2 tablespoons butter or
  margarine
¼ cup minced onion
8 ounce package cream cheese
1 cup sour cream
2 eggs
2 cups grated zucchini
Salt and pepper to taste
1 teaspoon dried dill or 1
  tablespoon fresh dill

Preheat oven to 350° F.

Heat butter and sauté onion for 5 minutes. Put into container of blender or food processor with cream cheese, sour cream, and eggs. Blend until smooth. Combine with zucchini. Season with salt and pepper. Stir in dill. Pour into 8 well-buttered custard cups, filling cups three-quarters full. Set cups in pan of hot water. Bake for 25-30 minutes until firm and slightly puffed.

Remove from oven and let stand 5 minutes. Turn out onto rounds of sautéed eggplant or large slices of tomato. Garnish with chopped parsley or a small amount of tomato sauce.

TURKEY ZUCCHINI CASSEROLE
Serves 6

2 cups grated zucchini
2 eggs
½ cup bread crumbs
Salt and freshly ground
  pepper to taste
3 tablespoons butter
2 tablespoons chopped onion
2 cups cooked turkey, coarsely
  chopped
½ cup chicken bouillon
½ cup heavy cream

Preheat oven to 325° F.

Mix zucchini with 1 egg and ¼ cup bread crumbs. Season with salt and pepper. Heat butter in heavy saucepan and sauté onion until limp — about 5 minutes. Stir in turkey. Add bouillon and cream and remaining crumbs. Cook until mixture is simmering. Add egg and cook until mixture thickens. Grease a 8½x5½x2½-inch loaf pan. Pack half of zucchini mixture into bottom of pan. Over this place turkey filling. Cover with remaining zucchini. Pack down well. Cover pan with foil. Set pan into larger pan of hot water. Bake for 45 minutes until firm. Loosen edges with knife and turn out onto serving platter. Garnish with strips of pimiento or serve with tomato sauce.

ZUCCHINI SAUCE

¼ cup vegetable oil
¼ cup butter
½ cup minced onion
1 clove garlic, mashed
½ cup green pepper, minced
1½ pounds zucchini, sliced
  thin
3 cups tomato puree
Salt to taste
Freshly ground pepper to taste

Heat oil and butter in heavy saucepan. Cook onions and garlic for 2 minutes. Add remaining ingredients. Cook over low heat, stirring frequently, for 30 minutes. Serve over a pasta — ziti or macaroni.

SALMON TIMBALES WITH ZUCCHINI SAUCE

Serves 4

Timbales:

2 tablespoons butter
2 tablespoons flour
1 cup milk
Salt to taste
Freshly ground pepper to taste
2 teaspoons snipped dill
1½ cups cooked salmon,
   flaked (canned or fresh)
¼ cup dry cracker crumbs
3 eggs

Preheat oven to 375° F.

Heat butter in saucepan. Add flour and cook, stirring, for 2 minutes. Add milk and cook, stirring, until thick and smooth. Remove from heat. Add seasonings. Mix in salmon and crumbs. Beat eggs lightly and add, blending well. Turn mixture into well-buttered custard cups (3½ inches wide by 2½ inches deep). Place cups in pan of hot water. Bake for 45-55 minutes until centers are firm.

Zucchini Sauce:

2 tablespoons butter
2 tablespoons flour
1 cup milk
Salt to taste
Freshly ground pepper to taste
2 cups zucchini puree
4 mushroom caps, sautéd until
   golden but firm

Heat butter in saucepan and add flour. Cook, stirring, for 2 minutes. Add milk and cook, stirring until thick. Season. Stir in zucchini. Spread mixture over bottom of buttered shallow baking dish. Unmold timbales onto zucchini and top each one with a mushroom cap. Reheat in a 350° F. oven for 20 minutes.

SPICY ZUCCHINI OAT BARS
About 1½ dozen

½ cup butter or margarine
1 cup brown sugar
2 eggs
1¼ cups rolled oats
2 cups grated zucchini
1½ cups unbleached flour
½ teaspoon salt
1 teaspoon baking soda
¼ cup plain yogurt
1 teaspoon vanilla

Preheat oven to 350° F.

Cream butter and sugar until smooth. Add eggs, one at a time, beating well. Put oats and zucchini into container of blender or food processor and blend until very finely chopped. Stir into creamed mixture. Combine dry ingredients and add to first mixture with yogurt. Stir in vanilla and mix thoroughly. Turn into greased 9x13-inch baking pan. Bake for 35 minutes. When cool, cut into bars.

Fruits

Apples

One pound equals 2 cups sauce.

METHOD: Put whole, washed apples into deep saucepan. Pour water or cider about ½-inch deep in bottom. Cover pan and set over medium heat. When apples have burst open (length of time depends on type of apple) put them through a food mill or Squeezo strainer.

It is possible to cook the apples, peeled and cored, and then put them into the blender or food processor. This is a matter of individual taste. The food mill method gives the sauce more texture and cooking the apples in their skins adds to the flavor.

Applesauce can be frozen or processed in a boiling water bath (10 minutes for pints and quarts). Always add a bit of salt. Sometimes lemon juice is needed for flavor. It is best to preserve the sauce without extra sugar or spices as those would limit its future uses in recipes.

We think of applesauce as an accompaniment to ham, pork, or sausage, or as a dessert in itself with crisp sugar cookies on the side. Actually applesauce combines well with many other fruits and vegetables — and seasonings. Mix it with horseradish and cream for a sauce for roast goose or add orange rind and brandy and cook it down to a thick butter to be served with a pork roast. Fold well-seasoned applesauce into beaten egg whites and some whipped cream and serve as a quick dessert. Applesauce and winter squash are natural partners spiced with ginger and nutmeg and baked to let the flavors blend. Substitute a cup of applesauce for the liquid in your favorite gingerbread recipe along with some raisins and candied citrus peels and a little brandy. Bake in a jelly roll pan and cut into squares — after spreading with a simple lemon icing.

GAME HENS WITH APPLE SPICE STUFFING
Serves 8

1 cup applesauce
Grated rind of 1 lemon
Juice of ½ lemon
1 tablespoon rum
1 teaspoon salt
¼ teaspoon each nutmeg,
   cinnamon, allspice, mace
2 cups stuffing bread cubes
4 Cornish game hens

Mix first seven ingredients together thoroughly. Stuff 4 game hens with mixture. Roast for 40 minutes at 350° F., basting with ½ cup melted butter, juice of 1 lemon, 2 tablespoons rum, and a dash of Tabasco.

QUICK APPLE LAMB CURRY
Serves 4-5

2 tablespoons vegetable oil
1 tablespoon butter
1 large onion, chopped
½ cup applesauce
1 teaspoon curry powder
2 cups cooked lamb, diced
2 cups chicken broth
Juice of ½ lemon
½ cup cream
Salt and pepper to taste

Heat oil and butter and sauté onion until soft. Stir in applesauce and curry powder and cook for 5 minutes. Stir in lamb. Add chicken broth and bring to a boil. Cover pan and reduce heat to simmer. Cook 30 minutes. Add lemon juice and cream. Bring to a boil and taste for seasoning.

Serve very hot over rice accompanied by chutney, sliced bananas, chopped bacon, green pepper, and hardcooked eggs.

APPLESAUCE CHEESE BREAD

One loaf

1 cup unbleached flour
1 cup whole wheat flour
1 teaspoon baking powder
1 teaspoon baking soda
1 teaspoon salt
½ cup butter or margarine
½ cup honey
2 eggs
1 cup unsweetened applesauce
½ cup grated sharp cheddar
   cheese
½ cup chopped walnuts

Combine flours, baking powder, soda, and salt. Cream honey and butter until well blended. Add eggs one at a time, beating well. Add applesauce alternately with dry ingredients. Stir in cheese and nuts. Mix well.

Turn into greased loaf pan. Leave the center slightly hollow. Bake at 350° F. for 1 hour. Turn out and cool on rack.

APPLE TOAD IN THE HOLE

Serves 2

1 cup applesauce
4 link sausages, cooked
½ cup milk
½ cup flour
2 eggs
½ teaspoon salt

Butter a 6-inch ovenproof dish or skillet. Put applesauce in bottom. Arrange sausages over sauce. Beat together the milk, flour, eggs, and salt. Pour over sausages. Bake in preheated 400° F. oven for 20-30 minutes until firm, puffed, and golden. Serve immediately.

APPLESAUCE WITH MAYONNAISE AND MINT

1 cup applesauce
2 sprigs mint
¼ cup cider or white wine
2 teaspoons freshly grated
  horseradish
½ cup mayonnaise
Salt to taste
Freshly ground pepper to taste
1 teaspoon Dijon mustard

Put applesauce into saucepan with cider or wine and mint. Simmer for 15 minutes until slightly reduced. Remove mint and cool. Stir in horseradish, mayonnaise, and seasonings. Chill. Serve with fish.

APPLESAUCE RING
Serves 6

1 envelope plain gelatin
¼ cup cold water
1 cup chicken broth
1 cup unsweetened applesauce
½ cup mayonnaise
½ cup sour cream
2 hardcooked egg yolks
Juice of ½ lemon
Curry powder to taste (about 1
  teaspoon)

Soften gelatin in cold water. Heat chicken broth and dissolve gelatin in it. Put gelatin mixture, applesauce, mayonnaise, sour cream, egg yolks, and lemon juice into container of blender or food processor. Blend for 30 seconds. Add about 1 teaspoon curry powder. Blend 5 seconds. Taste for strength of curry powder. Turn into ring mold and refrigerate until firm. Turn out onto serving platter and fill center with chicken or tuna salad.

APPLE BANANA GRAHAM BREAD

Two loaves

1 cup butter or margarine
1⅓ cups honey
4 eggs
2 ripe bananas, mashed
½ cup unsweetened
   applesauce
1½ cups unbleached flour
½ cup wheat germ
1 cup graham flour
3 teaspoons baking powder
1 teaspoon salt
½ cup buttermilk
1 teaspoon grated lemon rind
½ cup chopped nuts (optional)

Cream butter and honey. Add eggs, one at a time, beating well. Beat in bananas and applesauce. Combine dry ingredients and add to batter alternately with buttermilk. Stir in lemon rind and nuts. Turn into 2 well-greased 9x5-inch loaf pans. Bake at 350° F. for 50-60 minutes. Cool in pans on racks for 10 minutes. Remove from pans and cool before slicing.

DANISH APPLE CAKE

Serves 10-12

2 cups finely crushed
   zwieback crumbs
1 cup melted butter
¾ cup sugar
1 heaping teaspoon cinnamon
½ teaspoon ground cardamom
3 cups unsweetened
   applesauce
Whipped cream

Preheat oven to 350° F.

Mix crumbs and melted butter. Mix sugar and spices. Put thin layer of crumbs on bottom of buttered 9-inch tube pan. Sprinkle with sugar mixture. Add thin layer of applesauce. Repeat layers until ingredients are used up. Bake for 1 hour. Cool and turn out. Frost with whipped cream.

We all know about applesauce cake but what about substituting applesauce for the liquid in muffins and adding walnuts and dates? Or fold ½ cup applesauce into a stiffly beaten egg white and use it to top a caramel spice cake. Applesauce is number one on fall's hit parade.

ORANGE WHEAT CREPES
WITH APPLE FILLING
About 24 crepes

Crepes:

1 cup whole wheat flour
3 eggs
½ cup orange juice
½ cup + 2 tablespoons milk
2 tablespoons butter, melted
½ teaspoon salt
2 tablespoons brandy
  (optional)

Put all ingredients into blender or mixer and beat until smooth. Make crepes or very thin pancakes.

Filling:

2 cups thick applesauce
Brown sugar to taste
½ teaspoon cinnamon
½ teaspoon ginger
Grated rind of 1 orange

Sweeten applesauce to taste with sugar. Stir in remaining ingredients. Fill each crepe with 1-2 tablespoons mixture. Fold over and place in one layer in buttered shallow baking dish. Sprinkle with granulated sugar and melted butter. Glaze under broiler.

APPLE CIDER BREAD PUDDING
Serves 8

12 slices whole wheat bread
Butter
4 eggs
½ cup granulated sugar
½ cup brown sugar
1 tablespoon vanilla
1 teaspoon grated nutmeg
1 cup cider
2 cups milk
2 cups applesauce
Brandied whipped cream or
  custard sauce

Cut crusts off bread. Butter on one side and cut into ½-inch strips. Cover bottom of greased 2-quart baking dish with bread strips. Beat together next eight ingredients. Alternate layers of bread strips and egg mixture in dish. Place dish in pan of hot water. Bake at 325° F. for 1 hour or until pudding is firm and puffy. Serve with brandied whipped cream or custard sauce.

APPLE SCOTCH PIE
Serves 6

2 eggs, separated
1 cup dark brown sugar
3 tablespoons flour
¼ teaspoon salt
1 cup whole milk
¼ cup cream
1 tablespoon vanilla
½ cup applesauce
½ teaspoon grated nutmeg
Baked 9-inch pie shell
2 tablespoons sugar

In heavy saucepan put egg yolks, brown sugar, flour, salt, milk, and cream. Beat together with whisk. Cook over medium heat, stirring, until thick and smooth. Stir in vanilla. Mix applesauce with nutmeg and spread over bottom of pie shell. Spread custard mixture over applesauce.

Preheat oven to 350° F. Beat whites, gradually adding 2 tablespoons sugar. Beat until stiff and shiny. Spread over pie and bake for 15 minutes until meringue is brown.

APPLE TRIFLE
Serves 6

3 egg yolks
¼ cup sugar
1 cup half and half (cream and milk)
1 cup unsweetened applesauce
1 sponge cake
½ cup apricot preserve
⅓ cup sherry
1 cup heavy cream
4 tablespoons confectioners' sugar
1 teaspoon vanilla
¼ cup slivered almonds (optional)

Mix yolks and sugar in heavy saucepan. Gradually stir in half and half. Cook over medium heat, stirring, until mixture coats back of spoon. Pour into bowl and set bowl in pan of ice until chilled and thickened. Blend applesauce into custard.

Cut sponge cake into fingers 1-inch wide and 3-inches long. Spread with apricot preserve. Place half of sponge fingers in bottom of 10-inch glass bowl. Sprinkle with half of sherry. Cover with half of custard mixture. Whip cream with sugar and vanilla. Spread half over custard. Repeat with remaining ingredients. Sprinkle almonds over top. Refrigerate until serving time.

APPLESAUCE PIE
1 9-inch pie

2 cups applesauce
Juice and grated rind of ½ lemon
½ teaspoon mace
1 tablespoon melted butter
2 eggs, separated
⅓ cup sugar
1 9-inch unbaked pie shell
3 tablespoons sugar

Preheat oven to 425° F.

Mix together the applesauce, lemon rind and juice, mace, butter, egg yolks, and ⅓ cup sugar. Turn into pie shell. Bake for 10 minutes. Lower heat to 350° F. and bake for 20-23 minutes until filling is set. Beat egg whites until stiff, gradually adding 3 tablespoons sugar. Spread over pie filling and return to oven. Bake for 10 minutes until meringue is golden.

APPLE ANGEL PIE
Serves 6

4 egg yolks
½ cup sugar
Grated rind of 1 lemon
Grated rind of 1 orange
⅓ cup orange juice
1 cup applesauce
1 cup heavy cream
9-inch meringue nest

In heavy saucepan combine yolks and sugar. Mix well. Stir in grated rinds and orange juice. Cook, stirring, over medium heat until thick and smooth. Cool. Fold in applesauce.

Whip cream until stiff and spread half in meringue shell. Top with applesauce mixture. Cover with remaining cream. Refrigerate 2-3 hours before serving.

EASY APPLE GRAHAM PIE
Serves 6

¼ cup brown sugar
½ teaspoon cinnamon
½ teaspoon grated nutmeg
¼ teaspoon ground ginger
2 cups applesauce
1 cup heavy cream
2 tablespoons confectioners'
   sugar
1 teaspoon vanilla
1 9-inch baked graham cracker
   pie shell
¼ cup chopped walnuts

Stir brown sugar and spices into applesauce. Beat cream until stiff, adding confectioners' sugar and vanilla. Fold applesauce into cream and fill pie shell. Sprinkle with walnuts.

HOT APPLE MOUSSE
Serves 6

5 egg whites
1 cup cold applesauce,
    sweetened to taste
¼ cup granulated sugar mixed
    with ½ teaspoon cinnamon
Whipped cream

Preheat oven to 350° F.

Stir juice and cinnamon into applesauce. Mix with crumbs. Cream butter and sugar until well blended. Add salt and egg yolks and beat well. Combine with applesauce mixture. Beat whites until foamy. Add sugar gradually and beat until stiff and shiny. Fold into apple mixture. Turn into buttered 1-quart baking dish. Set dish in pan of hot water and bake for 1 hour or until puffed and firm. Serve warm with whipped cream.

APPLE CREAM
Serves 4-5

2 cups applesauce
½ cup white wine
1 2-inch piece cinnamon stick
3 whole cloves
1 strip lemon peel
1 cup heavy cream
Nutmeg

Put applesauce, wine, cinnamon, cloves, and lemon peel into saucepan. Simmer until mixture is quite thick. Cool. Remove spices.

Beat cream and fold in applesauce. Serve immediately sprinkled with freshly grated nutmeg.

You will find that a combination of apples is preferable in many recipes. Some are sweeter or more tart than others and there is certainly a difference in color. McIntosh give a pink cast and Russet add a lot of extra sugar. Experiment — you will find a favorite combination.

APPLE PUDDING
Serves 4-5

2 tablespoons orange juice or
  cider
1 teaspoon cinnamon
2 cups applesauce
½ cup cake crumbs
2 tablespoons butter
½ cup brown sugar
½ teaspoon salt
2 eggs, separated
3 tablespoons granulated
  sugar
Whipped cream

Preheat oven to 300° F.

Beat egg whites until stiff. Fold in applesauce. Shape on an ovenproof platter into a large oval egg — or any shape you wish to make. Sprinkle all over with sugar-cinnamon mixture. Bake for 35 minutes. Serve hot with whipped cream to which a little of the sugar-cinnamon mixture has been added.

APPLE CRISP PUDDING
Serves 4

2 cups granola-type cereal
2 cups applesauce
¼ cup brown sugar
2 tablespoons butter or
  margarine
1 teaspoon cinnamon
Vanilla ice cream

Put ½ cup cereal into bottom of greased baking dish. Cover with ½ cup applesauce. Repeat layers until ingredients are used up. Cream together the sugar, butter, and cinnamon. Dot top of pudding with mixture. Bake at 350° F. for 30 minutes. Serve with vanilla ice cream.

MERINGUE NESTS

About 8 small or 1 large nest

4 egg whites
¼ teaspoon salt
1¼ cups superfine sugar
1 teaspoon vanilla

Put whites into bowl of mixer with salt. Beat until stiff. Add sugar by spoonfuls, beating constantly until ¾ of sugar has been added. Fold in remaining sugar with vanilla. With a pastry tube or a spoon shape mixture into small nests or cups on lightly greased baking sheet. Bake at 200° F. for 45-60 minutes. Do not brown. Cool in oven with door open. Meringues should be crisp and dry to the touch.

APPLE CREAM PIE

⅔ cup sugar
2 tablespoons flour
¼ teaspoon salt
1 cup sour cream
1 egg
1 teaspoon vanilla
2 cups thick applesauce
1 9-inch unbaked pie shell
⅓ cup flour
⅓ cup brown sugar
¼ cup butter or margarine
1 teaspoon cinnamon

Combine sugar, flour, and salt. Beat in sour cream, egg, and vanilla. Fold in applesauce. Turn into pie shell. Combine flour, brown sugar, butter, and cinnamon and work with fingertips until crumbly. Sprinkle over top of filling. Bake at 400° F. for 30 minutes until firm.

Apricots

One pound apricots equals 1 cup puree.

METHOD: Dip fruit quickly into boiling water. Skin. Halve and remove pits. Puree in blender or food processor or put through food mill or Squeezo strainer. Add lemon juice or ascorbic acid. Freeze. To can, cook fruit and process in boiling water bath.

Thanks to our untiring professional agriculturists, the apricot is now a hardy tree and can be grown with great success in the northern climates. We have apricots to eat right from the tree, to use in soups, salads, main courses, and desserts, and to put up as puree if we wish. And we do wish because there are so many things you can do with this particular puree. The sweetened puree — and when it comes to sweetening I always beg the issue by saying "to your own taste" — is an excellent filling for a plain yellow cake. Because of its golden color it is the perfect accent in the middle of an almond butter cookie. Incidentally, almond is the best flavoring for apricot. Cupcakes hollowed out and filled with apricot are pleasantly surprising at tea time, and flaky biscuits with their own apricot sauce go over well with any meal.

Apricots are versatile — they do not necessarily have to go with sweets. With a bit of onion and some curry powder, apricot puree makes a good stuffing for pork chops and it gives a new twist to an old chicken dish. If you don't have an apricot tree, plant one.

APRICOT CAKE

1 8-inch cake

½ cup butter or margarine
1 cup sugar
2 egg yolks
1 teaspoon vanilla
½ teaspoon almond extract
1¾ cups cake flour
½ teaspoon salt
½ teaspoon soda
1 teaspoon baking powder
½ cup apricot puree
¼ cup orange juice

Preheat oven to 350° F.

Cream butter and sugar until light. Add egg yolks, one at a time, beating well. Add vanilla and almond extract. Combine flour with salt, soda, and baking powder. Add to creamed mixture alternately with apricot puree and orange juice. Turn into greased 8-inch square baking pan and bake for 40 minutes until cake tests done. Turn oven heat to broil. Spread almond frosting over cake and return to oven, broiling until lightly brown.

ALMOND FROSTING

6 tablespoons melted butter
1 cup brown sugar
¼ cup cream
1 cup slivered almonds

Mix all together and spread over top of just-baked cake.

GAME HENS WITH APRICOT SAUCE

Serves 4

2 Cornish game hens, 1½-2
    pounds apiece, cut in half
Salt to taste
Freshly ground pepper to taste
3 tablespoons butter
1 tablespoon lemon juice
1 cup apricot puree
½ cup orange juice
Grated rind of ½ orange
1 teaspoon ground ginger
¼ cup honey
1 tablespoon grated onion
Orange slices

Preheat broiler.

Arrange game hens, skin side up on broiler pan. Sprinkle with salt and pepper. Melt butter with lemon juice and brush birds with mixture. Broil 4 inches from heat until golden, basting with butter mixture. Turn and brush underside with it. Broil until lightly browned.

In a saucepan heat together the remaining ingredients, stirring until well blended. Turn oven to 350° F. Transfer game hens to buttered baking dish, skin side up. Pour apricot sauce over them. Cover with foil. Bake for 40 minutes. Serve garnished with orange slices and accompanied by rice with raisins and almonds.

APRICOT TEA BISCUITS

About 16 2-inch biscuits

2 cups apricot puree
½ cup sugar or to taste
2 tablespoons butter
½ teaspoon almond extract
2 cups all-purpose flour
4 teaspoons baking powder
1 tablespoon sugar
1 teaspoon salt
⅓ cup butter
Approximately ⅔ cup
    buttermilk
1 cup slivered toasted almonds

Preheat oven to 425° F.

To make filling, heat apricot puree with sugar and butter. Stir until well blended. Add almond extract. Cool. Put dry ingredients into mixing bowl and mix well. Cut in butter until mixture resembles coarse meal. Stir in buttermilk, mixing until dough is thoroughly blended. Turn out and knead for 2 minutes, adding flour if necessary. Dough should be soft but not sticky. Roll dough ½-inch thick. Cut with 2-inch cutter. Place biscuits on ungreased baking sheet. Bake for 15 minutes until delicately browned. Cool. Split biscuits in half and spread lower half with apricot filling. Put on top half and spread lightly with filling. Cover with almonds. Reheat at 400° F. for 6-7 minutes before serving.

Blackberries

Two cups equals 1 cup puree.

METHOD: Put blackberries into saucepan over low heat. Simmer until juice flows, about 10 minutes. Puree in blender or food processor. If you wish a seedless puree, put through a food mill. Sweeten to taste.

Berries are so perishable that, after we have eaten our fill in cakes, pies and puddings — and made jars of jam — it is nice to have another way to preserve them.

Berry puree freezes well and can be used any time during the winter to make jam or just sweetened for a cake filling. It goes nicely into turnovers for tea or muffins for breakfast or you might try spreading it on bread dough with a mixture of cinnamon and nuts, then rolling the dough and baking it as a loaf. Sherbets, ices, and mousses are all welcome summer desserts and a custard with blackberry caramel sauce could have its picture taken. It tastes good too.

BLACKBERRY CARAMEL CUSTARD

Serves 6-8

1 cup granulated sugar
½ cup blackberry puree
4 eggs
1 cup heavy cream
2 egg yolks
⅓ cup sugar
2½ cups milk
1 teaspoon vanilla
Fresh fruit

Preheat oven to 375° F.

Pour sugar into heavy skillet. Set over medium heat and cook, without stirring, until sugar is brown and syrupy. Shake pan back and forth over burner occasionally to spread sugar evenly over bottom of pan. When sugar has melted, add puree. Stir to mix and quickly pour into 1½-quart ring mold, tipping mold to coat sides. Use potholder gloves and be very careful as sugar can cause bad burns. Set mold aside to cool.

Scald cream. Put eggs, yolks, and the ⅓ cup sugar into mixing bowl. Beat until smooth. Beat in cream, milk, and vanilla. Pour into mold. Set mold in pan of hot water and cover with foil. Bake for 45-50 minutes until custard is firm.

Chill custard thoroughly. Run knife around edges and unmold onto serving platter. You may have to dip mold into hot water for a count of ten. Fill center with fresh fruit.

BLACKBERRY SHERBET

1 quart

2 cups blackberry puree
2 cups sugar
1½ cups milk
½ cup crème de cassis

Mix berry puree with sugar, milk, and cassis. Pour into container of ice cream freezer and freeze according to manufacturer's directions. Serve with raspberry sauce.

Blueberries

Two cups equal 1 cup puree.

METHOD: Put berries in saucepan over medium heat. Cook until juices run and berries burst. Put through food mill or Squeezo strainer, or puree in blender or food processor. If you wish a clear syrup, puree first, then put through finest blade of food mill. Sweeten to taste. Can be frozen or processed in hot water bath.

Perhaps the true essence of summer is best captured in the orchard produce — or at least that from the berry patch. Berries are so perishable they really should be eaten immediately so any method of preserving them is a plus. You should sweeten the puree while it is still warm — and all berries need some sugar whether or not they will be used for dessert. It heightens the natural flavor of the fruit.

Blueberry sauce takes naturally to lemon, either rind or juice, and cinnamon, either cooked with a piece of cinnamon bark or a whiff of ground cinnamon stirred in. I once had a wonderful blueberry sauce to which a tablespoon of gin had been added. It was served over banana fritters.

Blueberry sauce can be poured into muffin tins and covered with cupcake batter. Baked and unmolded you have ready-sauced little cakes which only need a dollop of cinnamon-flavored whipped cream to complete the picture. Blueberry sauce is lovely over lemon sherbet — or our lemon cheese pie. And I don't have to tell you what it does for pancakes and waffles.

BOOTHBAY BLUEBERRY SAUCE

About 1⅓ cups

1 cup blueberry puree
2 tablespoons sugar
2 tablespoons orange juice
1 tablespoon grated lemon
  rind
2 tablespoons grated orange
  rind
½ teaspoon allspice
½ teaspoon cinnamon

Combine all ingredients in saucepan and bring to a boil. Reduce heat and simmer for 10 minutes. Serve hot over ice cream, sponge cake, or fruit fritters.

CHEESE BARS WITH BLUEBERRY SAUCE

5 tablespoons butter or
  margarine
⅓ cup brown sugar
1 cup whole wheat flour
¼ cup chopped walnuts
½ cup granulated sugar
1 8-ounce package cream
  cheese
1 egg
2 tablespoons plain yogurt
Grated rind of 1 lemon
1 teaspoon vanilla
1 cup blueberry puree
1 tablespoon cornstarch
1 tablespoon cold water

Preheat oven to 350° F.

Cream together the butter and brown sugar. Beat in flour and nuts. Press mixture firmly into bottom of 9-inch square baking pan. Bake crust for 12 minutes. Remove from oven. Beat together the granulated sugar, cream cheese, egg, yogurt, lemon rind, and vanilla. Blend well. Pour over baked crust and return pan to oven. Bake for 25 minutes until firm. Heat blueberry puree in saucepan. Dissolve cornstarch in 1 tablespoon cold water and stir into blueberry puree. Cook, stirring, until thick and shiny. Pour over cheese mixture. Cool before cutting into bars.

Grapes

One pound equals 2 cups puree.

METHOD: With fingers squeeze pulp from skins. Put skins into bowl and pulp with seeds into saucepan. Heat pulp until soft and liquid. Put pulp into colander and push through into bowl containing skins, leaving seeds in colander. Freeze or can with sugar syrup in boiling water bath.

We grow table grapes, both red and white, and if we can get them before the birds do, we usually have a good supply. The Concord grapes seem to be our favorites, mainly because of their color which, when cooked, ranges from a vibrant lavender to a deep purple.

For a dessert that is spectacular in appearance, serve grape ice cream with a raspberry sauce — on pale pink or lavender plates if you have them. It is a once-a-fall feast and we look forward to it every year.

Grapes do go well with certain other fall fruits, especially cranberries, and in addition to desserts you can use them both with the heavier meats such as pork or venison. This combination in turn makes us think of the wines that marry well with these foods, Port and Madeira or a musky sherry. Try different combinations of these fruits and wines to see which appeal to your palate. It makes autumn eating something to look forward to.

RUTH ELLEN CHURCH'S GRAPE ICE CREAM

About 2½ cups

1½ cups grape puree, with
   skins
½ cup sugar
2 tablespoons light corn syrup
2 tablespoons lemon juice
¼ teaspoon salt
2 egg yolks
1 cup heavy cream

Put puree (including skins) into saucepan with sugar, corn syrup, lemon juice, and salt. Bring to a boil. Remove from heat and whisk in egg yolks, one at a time, working quickly. Return to heat and cook over medium heat, stirring constantly, for 3 minutes. Pour into a bowl and set bowl in pan of ice cubes. When cold, stir in cream. Fill container of ice cream machine and freeze according to manufacturer's directions. Serve with Cinnamon Plum Nut Sauce.

FRUIT GLAZED PORK CHOPS

Serves 6

6 lean ¾-inch thick pork
   chops
Salt to taste
Freshly ground pepper to taste
2 tablespoons shortening
1 cup grape puree
¾ cup port wine
½ cup sugar
½ cup fresh cranberries
1 tablespoon cornstarch
   dissolved in 1 tablespoon
   cold water

Preheat oven to 325° F.

Rub salt and pepper into both sides of chops. Heat shortening in heavy skillet and brown chops on both sides. Remove chops to casserole.

Pour grape puree and wine into skillet. Add sugar and bring to a boil, stirring. Add cranberries and cook for 4-5 minutes. Pour over pork chops. Cover casserole and bake for 45-50 minutes.

Remove chops to serving platter. Pour liquid from casserole into saucepan and put over medium heat. Stir in cornstarch and cook until smooth and thick. Pour over chops. This sauce will be purple in color so serve a harmonizing vegetable with it such as cabbage, yellow squash, or wax beans.

Peaches

One pound equals 1 cup puree.

METHOD: Scald peaches briefly in boiling water and peel off skins. Pit, dice, and puree in blender or food processor. Add lemon juice or ascorbic acid. Sweeten, freeze or bring puree to a boil and pack into jars. Process in boiling water bath.

Peach puree will stand on its own as a sauce for cakes or puddings and can be used nicely in muffins and cookies, replacing part of the liquid. Try a brandied peach cake and, if it is around long enough to get slightly tired, toast slices and spread them with peach jam for breakfast.

Like the apricot or nectarine, the peach can be used in a variety of ways and when you have a supply of dead-ripe peaches, the puree method prevents wasting any of this beautiful fruit. Peach ice creams, the kind made in molds or refrigerator trays, are so easy to do — perhaps the simplest possible dessert. It is just a matter of sweetening the puree, seasoning it with a little almond extract, and folding it into some stiffly whipped cream. If you wish to add ground almonds or crushed vanilla wafers you can. Freeze in a mold until firm, turn out and serve with fresh peach slices.

To get a little more involved, make a custard sauce with egg yolks and milk. Fold in the puree with a little chopped candied ginger. When it is cool, fold in whipped cream and beaten egg whites and turn the mixture into a soufflé dish. Chill.

PEACH SYLLABUB
Serves 6

4 egg yolks
⅓ cup sugar
½ cup peach puree
¼ cup Madeira wine
½ cup heavy cream

Put yolks in heavy saucepan. Using whisk, beat in sugar and peach puree. Cook over medium heat, stirring constantly, until slightly thickened. Add Madeira and cook, stirring, until mixture coats the back of a metal spoon. Put the spoon into the custard and run your fingertip down the back. If the mark leaves a "track," it is cooked.

Pour into a bowl and cool. Whip cream until stiff and fold into the cooled mixture. This can now be turned into parfait or dessert glasses and chilled, or used as a filling for a cake.

MELON CAKE
Serves 6

1 cup sugar
1 cup flour
1 teaspoon baking powder
½ teaspoon salt
2 large eggs
Heavy cream

Preheat oven to 350° F.

Put dry ingredients into mixing bowl. Break eggs into measuring cup and fill cup with heavy cream to make one cup liquid. Stir into dry ingredients, beating by hand until smooth. Pour into well-buttered and floured 1½-quart melon mold. Set mold on baking sheet and bake for 50 minutes until cake tests done in the middle and draws away at the sides. Let stand for 10 minutes. Run knife around edge of mold and unmold cake onto rack. Cool completely. Cut a 1½-inch slice off bottom of cake. Hollow out top rounded piece leaving about ½-inch around sides. Save crumbs for Apple Pudding. Fill with well-chilled Peach Syllabub. Put cake together and refrigerate on oven-proof plate. Just before serving, make a meringue by beating 2 egg whites until stiff with 4 tablespoons sugar. Spread over entire outside of cake and bake for 12-15 minutes, or until browned. Serve immediately.

CHICKEN IN PEACH SAUCE

Serves 4

1 teaspoon salt
Freshly ground pepper to taste
1 teaspoon paprika
1 3-pound frying chicken, cut
   into serving pieces
1 tablespoon salad oil
3 tablespoons butter
½ cup chicken bouillon
1 medium onion, chopped
Juice of ½ lemon
½ cup peach puree
2 tablespoons sugar
¼ cup white wine
Broiled peach halves

Rub salt, pepper, and paprika into chicken pieces. Heat oil and 2 tablespoons butter in large skillet. Brown chicken on all sides. Pour in bouillon, bring to a boil. Cover and reduce heat. Simmer for 20 minutes. Meanwhile, heat remaining tablespoon butter in skillet and sauté onion until soft, about 5 minutes. Add lemon juice, peach puree, and sugar. Cook, stirring, for 5 minutes. Add wine and bring to a boil. Pour over chicken and cook for 20 minutes longer. Arrange chicken on serving platter with sauce and surround with broiled peach halves.

BRANDY PEACH CAKE

1 8-inch square cake

½ cup butter or margarine
½ cup brown sugar
½ cup granulated sugar
1 egg
1 teaspoon baking soda
½ teaspoon salt
1 cup peach puree
1¾ cups flour
⅓ cup peach brandy

Preheat oven to 350° F.

Cream butter and sugars together until smooth and light. Beat in egg. Add baking soda and salt to peach puree. Add flour and puree alternately to creamed mixture. Stir in brandy. Blend well. Turn into greased 8x8-inch square baking pan. Bake for 40 minutes until cake tests done. When cool, sprinkle with powdered sugar.

Pears

One pound equals 1 cup puree.

METHOD: Peel and core pears. Dice and puree in blender or food processor. Pour puree into saucepan and add lemon juice. Sweeten to taste and heat until sugar is dissolved. Cool and freeze or pour hot into jars and process in boiling water bath.

We start with the Bartletts, which we do not puree because they are perfect eating pears as they are, and they ripen so quickly. Also, we feel that the later varieties have a more definite flavor and can take spices and stronger seasonings. Incidentally, pears ripen from the inside out so when they show dark spots on the outside, they will be overripe. Gentle pressure on the stem end will tell the state of ripeness.

PEAR PEANUT BUTTER SQUARES
9 squares

¾ cup pear puree
⅓ cup granulated sugar
⅓ cup brown sugar, packed
⅓ cup butter or margarine
⅓ cup peanut butter
1 egg
¾ cup unbleached flour
¼ teaspoon baking powder
½ teaspoon baking soda
¼ teaspoon salt

Preheat oven to 350° F.

Cream together the pear puree, sugars, butter, and peanut butter until smooth and well blended. Beat in egg. Combine remaining ingredients and stir in. Turn into greased 9-inch square baking pan. Bake for 25 minutes. Cool. Cut into 9 squares.

GINGER PEAR SAUCE
About 6 pints

6 pounds ripe pears
1 pound crystallized ginger, chopped fine
6 cups sugar
Grated rind and juice of 3 lemons

Cut pears in half and remove cores and stems. Peel. Put into large saucepan with ginger, sugar, lemon juice, and rind. Cook uncovered over medium heat until soft. Depending on condition of pears this will take from 30 to 45 minutes. Put through food mill or food processor. Return to saucepan and cook until thickened.

Pears and chocolate, pears and ginger, pears and orange, pears and peanut butter — they are a very agreeable fruit. You could probably incorporate pears into every course of a meal, starting with soup, and not repeat your combination of seasonings. Try it.

PORK LOIN WITH PEAR SAUCE

Serves 6

1 pork loin, about 4 pounds,
  trimmed of excess fat
Salt to taste
Freshly ground pepper to taste
1 cup ginger pear sauce
¼ cup frozen orange juice
  concentrate
2 tablespoons soy sauce
1 small clove garlic, crushed
1 cup fresh pears, peeled and
  sliced

Preheat oven to 325° F.

Place pork roast in roasting pan on rack and sprinkle with salt and pepper. Roast for 1 hour. Put pear sauce, orange juice concentrate, soy sauce, and garlic in saucepan and bring to a boil, stirring. Spoon half of mixture over roast at end of first hour. Roast 20 minutes longer. Cover with remaining sauce and roast 20 minutes more. Add sliced pears to pan and roast 10 minutes. Slice and serve garnished with pears and sauce.

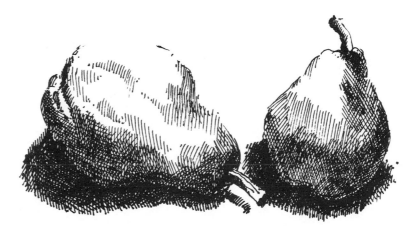

Plums

One pound equals 1 cup puree.

METHOD: Cut plums in half and remove pits. Puree in blender or food processor. Pour puree into saucepan and add 1 tablespoon sugar. Heat until sugar is dissolved. Freeze or process in boiling water bath.

Plum ice cream comes down from colonial days, and plum custard spiked with rum is far from invalid's fare. Naturally, plum sauce can be used in tarts and cakes, p.145, but have you ever tried it as one of the sauces for a beef fondu? It is a nicely surprising addition, along with the usual Béarnaise, tomato, and horseradish. Luckily the plum season is fairly long so we have time to choose and taste-test our favorites and puree the ones we like best. If you season at the same time you puree, note it on the jar labels. Plum sauce flavored with garlic does not do much for a layer cake.

DESSERT CAKE WITH PLUM SAUCE
Serves 8

½ cup butter or margarine
1 cup sugar
2 eggs
1½ cups flour
2 teaspoons baking powder
½ teaspoon salt
½ cup milk
1 teaspoon vanilla

Preheat oven to 350° F.

Cream butter and sugar until light. Beat in eggs, one at a time. Blend well. Combine dry ingredients and beat in alternately with milk. Stir in vanilla. Turn into 2 well-greased and floured 8-inch cake pans. Bake on middle rack of oven for 30 minutes until cake tests done. Let stand for 5 minutes. Turn out onto racks to cool.

1 cup or 10-ounce jar currant jelly
2 cups plum puree
2 tablespoons dry white wine

In saucepan combine jelly, plum puree, and wine. Cook over low heat, stirring, until jelly is melted and ingredients are well blended and thick. Spoon half of the mixture over one cake layer. Top with remaining layer. Spoon remaining sauce over top.

NIKA'S PLUM SAUCE
1½ cups

Excellent as a sauce for beef fondu or with shish kebab.

1½ cups plum puree
4 large garlic cloves, minced
Salt to taste
Freshly ground pepper to taste

Put puree in a saucepan and add garlic, salt, and pepper. Bring to a boil. Reduce heat and simmer 5 minutes, stirring frequently. Serve at room temperature.

Plums come in all sizes and colors but basically they can all be used for the same thing. The puree can be combined with red wine or Madeira and used in beef stew or it can be mixed with onion, garlic, and herbs to sauce pork. It will also go with chicken or veal.

PLUM DESSERT SAUCE
About 1½ cups

1½ cups plum puree
2 tablespoons sugar
¼ cup port wine
1 tablespoon cornstarch
2 tablespoons grated orange
   rind

Stir sugar into puree. Heat, stirring, until bubbling. Dissolve cornstarch in wine and stir into hot mixture. Cook, stirring, until slightly thickened and smooth. Stir in orange rind. Serve warm or cold over poached peaches or pears or hot winter puddings.

CINNAMON PLUM NUT SAUCE

2 cups plum puree
1 cup sugar
1 stick cinnamon
1 tablespoon cornstarch
2 tablespoons lemon juice
2 tablespoons water
½ cup chopped walnuts

In saucepan combine plum puree, sugar, and cinnamon stick. Simmer for 10 minutes. Mix cornstarch with lemon juice and water. Stir into sauce. Cook, stirring, until sauce thickens. Stir in nuts. Remove cinnamon stick. Serve warm.

Raspberries

Three cups berries equal 1½ cups puree.

METHOD: Put berries into saucepan and heat gently until juices run. Puree in blender or food processor. For a seedless puree, put through food mill or Squeezo strainer. Sweeten to taste. Freeze or process in boiling water bath. (Color remains brighter with freezing.)

Raspberries come in two seasons and many times the fall crop is better than the early summer crop. Then we can have our sauce over strawberries, peaches, nectarines, and even pears — and a beautiful sauce it is. There is nothing to equal the deep jewel ruby color of a raspberry puree.

Raspberry muffins are a good breakfast surprise, and raspberry puree over strawberry shortcake is unexpectedly delicious.

Try a rhubarb and raspberry fool by combining both pureed fruits with sweetened stiffly whipped cream. Raspberry sponge, raspberry custard, raspberry cream, raspberry parfait, raspberry pudding — those are the sweets. Then try raspberry sauce for game — rabbit or duck or small birds. You'll be wishing for a late frost so your raspberry sauce cookery can go on and on.

RABBIT WITH RASPBERRY SAUCE
Serves 4-5

1 3-4 pound rabbit, cut into
  serving pieces
½ cup flour
1 teaspoon salt
1 tablespoon paprika
2 tablespoons oil
2 tablespoons butter
½ medium onion, minced
1 cup beef bouillon
1 cup raspberry puree
2 tablespoons raspberry or
  currant jelly
1 tablespoon vinegar

Preheat oven to 350° F.

Dredge pieces of rabbit with flour, salt, and paprika. Heat oil and butter in large skillet and brown rabbit on all sides. Remove to baking dish. Add onion to skillet and sauté until soft, about 5 minutes. Add bouillon to skillet and bring to a boil, stirring up browned bits on bottom. Pour over rabbit. Cover dish and bake for 45 minutes or until rabbit is tender.

Remove rabbit to serving dish. Pour liquid in pan into saucepan. Add raspberry puree, jelly, and vinegar. Bring to a boil, stirring, and cook until smooth. Pour over rabbit and serve with parsleyed noodles.

RASPBERRY SPONGE
Serves 4

1 package unflavored gelatin
¼ cup cold water
2 cups raspberry puree
1 cup water
½ cup sugar or to taste
3 egg whites

Soak gelatin in cold water. Heat raspberry puree and 1 cup water with sugar, stirring until sugar dissolves. Taste for sweetness. Dissolve gelatin in very hot liquid. Cool until the consistency of egg white. Beat egg whites until stiff and fold into raspberry mixture. Turn into 1½-quart mold and chill until firm. Serve with whipped cream and thin sugar cookies.

Rhubarb

One pound equals 2 cups.

METHOD: Cut rhubarb stalks into 1-inch lengths. Put into heavy saucepan with one-fourth as much sugar as fruit. Cook, covered, over low heat until rhubarb is very soft. Puree in blender or food processor or put through fine blade of food mill and strain to obtain a clear syrup. Freeze or process in boiling water bath.

When a professional cooking friend asked me what my latest project was and I replied "garden sauces," she immediately said "Rhubarb sauce for ice cream? Divine!" And she's right. It's one of those superb combinations, especially with a sprinkling of chopped candied ginger over the top. No matter what the end result is, rhubarb has to be cooked with some sugar to begin with. Then you can add orange or lemon rind, ginger or cinnamon, vinegar and onion.

Rhubarb syrup with iced tea and a sprig of mint is a pleasant summer drink as is a rhubarb punch with lemon and orange juice and soda water. And if rhubarb sauce is good on ice cream why wouldn't a rhubarb ice cream soda be good also? We like a rhubarb pudding cake which calls for a plain yellow cake batter poured into a 9-inch square pan and hot rhubarb sauce poured over the batter. Then bake for about 40 minutes and you have a pre-sauced cake.

RHUBARB AND STRAWBERRY FOOL
Serves 6

2 cups rhubarb sauce
1 cup strawberry puree
1 cup sugar
1 cup heavy cream, whipped

Mix together the rhubarb and strawberry sauces. Sweeten to taste with sugar. Chill mixture. Fold in whipped cream gently so fruit forms ribbons through cream. Serve immediately.

SUSAN'S SPECIAL RHUBARB PUDDING
Serves 6

4 tablespoons butter
½ cup sugar
1 cup milk
1 cup flour
2 teaspoons baking powder
½ teaspoon salt
½ teaspoon ground ginger
4 cups rhubarb sauce,
   sweetened to taste
2 tablespoons brown sugar
Grated rind of ½ lemon
1 teaspoon cinnamon
½ teaspoon ground nutmeg

Preheat oven to 350° F.

Cream together the butter and sugar. Add milk. Combine flour, baking powder, salt, and ginger and stir in. Pour rhubarb into buttered 1½-quart baking dish. Put batter over top. Combine brown sugar, lemon rind, cinnamon, and nutmeg and sprinkle over batter. Bake for 30-35 minutes. Serve warm with cream.

RHUBARB CHARLOTTE

Serves 6

2 packages unflavored gelatin
½ cup orange juice
3 cups sweetened rhubarb
   puree
2 tablespoons orange
   marmalade (can use ginger
   or lemon marmalade)
¾ cup cream, whipped

Soften gelatin in orange juice. Dissolve by placing cup in pan of boiling water until clear and liquid. Stir together the gelatin, rhubarb, and marmalade. Chill mixture and when it is the consistency of egg white, fold in whipped cream. Turn into 5-cup mold and chill for several hours until set.

RHUBARB SANGRIA RING

Serves 6

2 packages unflavored gelatin
1 cup orange juice
2 cups rhubarb syrup
½ cup sugar
2 cups red wine
¼ cup orange liqueur
Strawberries

Soak gelatin in orange juice until firm. Heat rhubarb syrup with sugar. Dissolve soaked gelatin in very hot syrup. Combine with wine and liqueur. Pour into rinsed 1½-quart ring mold. Refrigerate for several hours or overnight. Turn out and fill center with strawberries. Serve as a dessert with almond cookies.

An excellent sauce for meats is made by cooking together until thick 4 cups rhubarb, ½ medium onion chopped, 1 cup chopped raisins, 1½ cups brown sugar, and ¼ cup vinegar. Then you add 1 teaspoon pumpkin pie spice and cook just to blend.

Strawberries

Three cups equals 2 cups puree.

METHOD: Hull strawberries and put into saucepan. Heat for 5 minutes or until juice starts to run. Puree in blender or food processor. Sweeten to taste. Freeze or can in boiling water bath. (Canning will take away bright color.)

Again, a berry that should be used at the peak of ripeness and one that has so much going for it that it is hard to stop listing ways to use it. Strawberry tops cheesecakes, meringues, cream puffs, pound cakes, and pies. The puree combines with butter to make strawberry butter for biscuits, pancakes, and waffles. It blends with ginger ale for a summer drink and with sugar, lemon juice, and orange liqueur for a frozen ice.

Fold strawberry puree into a recipe for nut bread or pour it over Indian pudding or layer it with frozen custard in parfait glasses. Beat it into butter-sugar icing for a cake. Combine it with rum and use it for sauce for poached peaches. Make a strawberry soup or a strawberry fool. Make a lot of strawberry puree and you'll be glad that you did.

YOGURT CHEESE WITH STRAWBERRY SAUCE

Serves 6

1 cup cottage cheese
2 tablespoons grated orange rind
2 tablespoons orange juice
⅓ cup honey
1 cup plain yogurt
1 cup strawberry sauce for topping

Put first five ingredients into container of blender or food processor. Blend until smooth. Turn into a bowl and put in freezer. Freeze until edges are firm and center is mushy. Take out and beat until smooth. Turn into a rinsed 2-cup mold, ring mold or 6 individual molds. Freeze solid. Unmold onto serving platter and cover with 1 cup strawberry sauce.

STRAWBERRY NECTARINE TART

Serves 6

1 cup strawberry puree
¼ cup currant or raspberry jelly
1 tablespoon cornstarch
1 8-ounce package cream cheese
½ cup sugar
Grated rind of ½ lemon
3 tablespoons frozen orange juice concentrate
2 cups peeled nectarine slices
1 8-inch baked tart shell (see page 70)

Heat together over medium heat the strawberry puree, jelly and cornstarch. Stir constantly until mixture thickens and is smooth. Remove from heat.

Beat together the cream cheese, sugar, lemon rind, and orange juice concentrate. Spread cream cheese mixture in tart shell. Arrange nectarine slices in a decorative pattern over cream cheese. Spread strawberry sauce over top. Chill.

AN ADULT RICE PUDDING
Serves 4

⅓ cup long grain rice (not
  minute rice)
1½ cups whole milk
½ teaspoon vanilla
1 teaspoon rum
¼ cup butter
2 eggs, separated
1 tablespoon sugar
1 cup strawberry puree,
  sweetened to taste
¼ cup ground almonds

Preheat oven to 350° F.

Put rice and milk in deep saucepan and bring to a boil. Reduce heat to low, cover pan, and let boil until rice is tender and milk is absorbed, about 20 minutes. Stir in vanilla and rum. Cool to lukewarm.

Cream butter and beat in yolks. Beat until mixture is smooth. Beat in sugar and rice mixture. Beat whites until stiff and fold in.

Butter well a 1-quart soufflé or baking dish. Combine almonds and strawberry puree and turn into bottom of dish. Pour rice mixture over top. Set dish in pan of hot water and cover loosely with waxed paper. Bake for 50-60 minutes, until firm in center. Remove and run knife around edge of dish. Unmold onto serving platter. Serve warm or at room temperature with whipped cream.

STRAWBERRY BATTER CUPS
Serves 8

1½ cups flour
½ teaspoon salt
1½ teaspoons baking powder
1 tablespoon butter or
  margarine
2 eggs
1 cup milk
4 cups strawberry puree
1 cup sugar or to taste

Preheat oven to 350° F.

Combine dry ingredients in bowl. Cut in butter. Beat in eggs and milk. Sweeten puree with sugar to taste. Butter well 8 custard cups. Place a thin layer of batter in each one, then a layer of strawberry puree. Repeat until cups are two-thirds full. Set cups on baking sheet and bake for 30-40 minutes until dough is firm and flaky. Turn cups out onto serving platter and serve with strawberry sauce.

FROZEN STRAWBERRY PARFAIT
Serves 6

3 egg yolks
4 tablespoons confectioners'
 sugar
¼ cup orange liqueur
1½ cups cream, whipped
2 cups strawberry puree,
 sweetened
Fresh strawberries, stemmed

Beat yolks and sugar until thick and creamy. Beat in liqueur by the spoonful, slowly. Fold in whipped cream. Spoon layers of cream, puree, and fresh strawberries into parfait glasses and freeze.

STRAWBERRY SAUCE

2 cups sugar
1 cup butter
2 egg whites
2 cups strawberry puree

Cream together the butter and sugar until very light. Beat in egg whites and strawberry puree. Chill.

Nuts

Almonds

One pound equals 2 cups ground nuts.

METHOD: Put nuts into container of blender or food processor and grind using on-off method with motor. Or grind with a hand grater. Freeze or store in refrigerator.

> I have never forgotten the first time I walked on almonds. It was in a grove in California and the ground was strewn with nuts that crunched and cracked as we walked along. Being a New Englander, my parsimonious soul was bothered by such seeming extravagance, but I managed to refrain from filling my pockets and instead thought of all the glorious things I could make with those almonds.
>
> They can be incorporated into soups and sandwich spreads. They can be used for coating foods to be fried or sautéd, either alone or combined with bread crumbs. Almonds enhance almost all fruits, especially a hot compote of canned apricots, Bing cherries, oranges, bananas, and pineapple all warmed in their juices with the addition of honey, port wine, and grated fruit rinds. They are very good sprinkled over seafood or chicken, and combine well with strawberries and peaches. If you are using almonds in a dessert, add a little almond extract to bring out the flavor of the nuts.

SHRIMP IN ALMOND SAUCE
Serves 4

2 tablespoons butter
1 tablespoon oil
1 onion, chopped
½ teaspoon garlic puree
2 cups tomato puree
½ cup minced parsley
Salt to taste
Freshly ground pepper to taste
½ teaspoon sugar
½ cup almonds
1½ pounds cooked, shelled
   shrimp

Heat butter and oil and sauté onion and garlic puree until limp but not browned, about 5 minutes. Stir in tomato puree and parsley. Season with salt and pepper. Stir in sugar and almonds. Simmer for 10 minutes. Add shrimp and heat but do not boil. Serve over rice.

GAZPACHO WITH ALMONDS
Serves 4

3 ripe peeled tomatoes
2 green peppers, seeds and
   membranes removed,
   chopped
1 sweet red pepper, seeds and
   membranes removed,
   chopped
½ large cucumber, peeled and
   seeded
1 slice bread
¼ cup finely ground almonds
Salt to taste
Freshly ground pepper to taste
1¾ cups chicken bouillon
¼ cup vinegar
2 tablespoons mayonnaise

Put tomatoes, peppers, cucumbers, and bread into container of blender or food processor and blend until smooth. Pour into bowl and mix in remaining ingredients. Chill for 1 hour. Serve in soup bowls to be garnished with croutons, chopped cucumber, tomato, and green pepper.

160

Pecans

One pound equals 2 cups ground nuts.

METHOD: Put nuts, a small amount at a time, into container of blender or food processor and grind, turning motor on and off quickly several times. Or grind nuts with hand grinder. Freeze or refrigerate.

The pecan is a native American nut, indigenous to our southern states, and its distinct flavor adds a lot to many dishes that might otherwise be rather dull. For instance, your leftover turkey hash — sauté finely chopped pecans and add to the basic hash mixture. Or begin at the beginning and add the pecans to the stuffing. Sprinkle pecans over pie crust for any fruit pie before filling and use them as a coating for croquettes or fritters. Ground pecans can also be used in place of flour as a thickener in many recipes (our pecan roll) or as a topping for soups (onion) or soufflés (chocolate).

VIRGINIA'S PECAN PUDDING
Serves 10

9 ounces vanilla wafers
½ cup butter
1 cup sugar
4 eggs
1 cup ground pecans
1 cup bourbon whiskey
Whipped cream

Grind vanilla wafers in blender or food processor until they are fine crumbs. Cream butter and sugar until light. Beat in eggs one at a time, mixing well. Beat in pecans and bourbon. Butter 1-quart soufflé dish and layer wafer crumbs and butter mixture alternately. Refrigerate for 48 hours. Serve with whipped cream piped on top.

CISSIE'S PECAN ROLL
Serves 10

7 eggs, separated
¾ cup sugar
2 cups ground pecans
1 teaspoon baking powder
Confectioners' sugar
1½ cups heavy cream,
   whipped

Preheat oven to 350° F.

Beat yolks, gradually adding sugar, until pale and light. Beat in 1½ cups of the pecans and the baking powder. Grease a 10x15-inch jelly roll pan. Line pan with waxed paper and grease paper. Beat whites until stiff and fold into pecan mixture. Spread mixture in pan. Bake for 18 minutes. Turn out onto clean towel. Let rest for 5 minutes. Strip off waxed paper. Sprinkle with confectioners' sugar. Roll up. Unroll and cool. Spread with sweetened whipped cream. Roll up and sprinkle with confectioners' sugar and remaining pecans.

EGGPLANT WITH PECAN SAUCE
Serves 4

8 1-inch thick slices of
   eggplant, peeled or not,
   according to taste
¼ cup flour
6 tablespoons butter
4 tablespoons oil
Salt to taste
Freshly ground pepper to taste
¾ cup medium or heavy cream
1½ cups ground pecans

Preheat oven to 375° F.

Dust eggplant slices with flour. Heat 4 tablespoons of the butter and the oil in skillet. Sauté eggplant until browned on both sides. Remove to greased shallow baking dish. Season with salt and pepper. Put 1½ tablespoons cream on each slice. Sprinkle pecans over all. Dot with remaining 2 tablespoons butter. Bake for 10-15 minutes until nuts are slightly toasted. Serve with fried chicken or veal. This also makes an interesting luncheon dish served with a salad.

Walnuts

One pound equals 2 cups.

METHOD: Put walnuts into blender, food processor, or hand grater a small amount at a time. Blend by turning motor on and off quickly several times. You do not want to release the oils in the nuts or you will produce nut butter. Store in refrigerator or freezer.

Walnuts are probably the most versatile of all of the nut family. A container of ground walnuts is a handy thing to have, as they can be sprinkled over almost anything and will add to the flavor and texture immeasurably. They are very good mixed with the aioli sauce and served with shrimp. The late Albert Stockli used them with sautéd zucchini. They also go well with green beans in lemon butter.

A very easy hors d'oeuvre is made from cheddar cheese mixed with chile peppers, parsley, pimiento, garlic, Worcestershire, butter, and brandy, then formed into a log and rolled in walnuts. There are many versions of the chicken with walnut sauce. One of the most impressive calls for decorating the finished dish with a pattern of paprika and walnut oil dribbled over the top at random (1 tablespoon paprika to ¼ cup oil). When you need to decorate a dish, or cover up mistakes, reach for the ground walnuts.

CHICKEN WITH WALNUT SAUCE

Serves 6

3 slices bread, crusts removed
2½ cups chicken bouillon, lukewarm
2 cups ground walnuts
Salt to taste
1-2 tablespoons paprika
3 whole chicken breasts, split, boned, skinned, and cooked. Do not chill.

Soak bread in ½ cup of the chicken bouillon and squeeze dry. Put bread and nuts into container of blender or food processor and blend until just mixed together. Turn into bowl and add salt and 1 tablespoon paprika. Beat in remaining bouillon, adding liquid gradually until sauce is consistency of a thin mayonnaise. Arrange chicken breasts on serving platter and spread sauce over them. Sprinkle with remaining paprika. Serve at room temperature.

COLD WALNUT SOUFFLÉ

Serves 6

⅔ cup granulated sugar
⅔ cup finely ground walnuts
4 eggs
4 tablespoons strong coffee
1 cup heavy cream
1 cup sour cream
⅔ cup confectioners' sugar
1 tablespoon rum

Put granulated sugar into heavy skillet over medium heat. Cook, shaking pan occasionally, until sugar is brown and syrupy. Stir nuts into syrup and pour mixture out onto a piece of aluminum foil. When hard, pulverize in blender or food processor. Put eggs and coffee (save from your morning brew) in top of double boiler over hot water. Beat until pale and thick. Cool. Whip heavy cream and fold into sour cream. Stir in confectioners' sugar and rum and fold into yolk mixture. Fold in half of walnut mixture. Turn into 1½-quart soufflé dish. Sprinkle with remaining walnut mixture. Chill 2-3 hours until firm.

WALNUT RAISIN SAUCE

About 3 cups

¼ cup vinegar
1¾ cups water
½ cup brown sugar
½ tablespoon mustard
½ tablespoon flour
1 tablespoon butter
1 teaspoon Worcestershire
   sauce
½ cup raisins
½ cup chopped walnuts

Heat together the vinegar, water, and sugar. Cook until sugar is dissolved. Combine mustard and flour. Moisten with liquid and stir into hot liquid over medium heat. Add butter and Worcestershire and cook until syrupy. Stir in raisins and walnuts. Serve with tongue or ham.

Gravies

VEAL IN WHITE WINE

Serves 6

2 tablespoons vegetable oil

3 tablespoons butter

2 medium carrots, scrubbed and diced

1 stalk celery, diced

1 medium onion, chopped

½ cup flour

1 teaspoon salt

2 teaspoons paprika

2 pounds lean veal, cut in 1-inch cubes

1 cup chicken bouillon

½ cup dry white wine or vermouth

Juice of ½ lemon

1 tablespoon chopped dill weed

Salt and freshly ground pepper to taste

2 tablespoons chopped parsley

2 teaspoons cornstarch (optional)

1 tablespoon cold milk (optional)

Preheat oven to 325° F.

In large skillet heat oil and butter. Sauté carrots, celery, and onion over medium heat for 4-5 minutes. Remove to deep casserole. Put flour, salt, and paprika in bag and shake veal cubes in mixture, coating each one. Brown veal in remaining fat in skillet. Add to casserole. Pour bouillon and wine into skillet. Bring to a boil, scraping brown bits off bottom of pan. Add lemon juice and dill and pour over veal. Season to taste with salt and pepper. Cover and bake for 1½ hours until veal is very tender. Remove veal to serving dish with slotted spoon and pour liquid and vegetable into container of blender or food processor. Blend until smooth. Pour over veal and sprinkle with parsley.

Note: If you wish to thicken sauce, mix 2 teaspoons cornstarch with 1 tablespoon cold milk and stir into sauce over heat before pouring over meat.

CHICKEN IN CURRIED APPLESAUCE
Serves 4

2 tablespoons butter or
    margarine
1 tablespoon vegetable oil
1 frying chicken, cut into
    serving pieces
Salt to taste
Freshly ground pepper to taste
1 teaspoon curry powder
½ teaspoon ground ginger
2 tablespoons chopped onion
½ cup chicken bouillon
2 tart apples, peeled and sliced
¼ cup roasted peanuts

Preheat oven to 350° F.

Heat oil and butter in skillet. Season chicken with salt and pepper and sauté in skillet until browned on all sides. Remove to deep casserole.

Add curry powder and ginger to skillet and cook, stirring, for 2 minutes. Add onion and bouillon and cook for 5 minutes. Pour over chicken. Add apples and peanuts to casserole. Cover and cook for 45 minutes. Remove chicken to heated serving platter. Put remaining contents of casserole, including apples and peanuts, into container of blender or food processor. Puree and pour over chicken. Serve with chutney.

FISH IN HERBED TOMATO SAUCE
Serves 6

Vegetable oil
2 tomatoes, skinned and
    chopped
3 tablespoons parsley
1 onion, minced
1 green pepper, diced
2 pounds haddock, cod, or
    halibut
Salt to taste
Freshly ground pepper to taste
Juice of ½ lemon
Paprika
1 tablespoon butter

Preheat oven to 400° F.

Pour a light film of oil over bottom of shallow baking dish. Put tomatoes, parsley, onion, and green pepper in dish. Set fish on top of vegetables. Sprinkle fish with salt, pepper, lemon juice, and paprika. Dot with 1 tablespoon butter. Bake for 25 minutes until fish tests done. Remove fish to serving platter.

Put vegetables into container of blender or food processor. Puree. Taste for seasoning and pour over fish.

Index